Looking Back on Progress

LORD NORTHBOURNE

Looking Back on Progress

Edited by
Christopher James
5th Lord Northbourne

Angelico Press
Sophia Perennis

First edition 1970 Perennial Books, Pates Manor
Second edition 1995, Sophia Perennis, Ghent
Revised and expanded edition, 2024
Angelico Press/Sophia Perennis

© Christopher James Northbourne 2001

All rights reserved

General editor: James R. Wetmore

No part of this book may be reproduced or transmitted,
in any form or by any means, without permission.

For information, address:
Angelico Press,
169 Monitor St.
Brooklyn, NY 11222
angelicopress.com

ISBN 978-0-900588-03-7 (pb)
ISBN 978-0-900588-53-2 (cloth)
ISBN 979-8-89280-055-6 (ebook)

Cover design: Michael Schrauzer

Contents

Foreword 1
I   Introductory 3
II   Pictures of the Universe 20
III   The Beauty of Flowers 40
IV   Being Oneself 58
V   Predestination & Free Will 63
VI   Planning for Progress 79
VII   A Glance at Agriculture 92
VIII   Old Age 110
IX   'With God All Things Are Possible' 117
Index 129

Foreword

Born in 1898, my father fought in the First World War. Amongst other things, he was with General Allenby and his contingent of Indian Muslim troops as they took Palestine from the Turks in 1918. The British decided to send in Muslim troops out of respect for the Palestinian population. He returned to study Agriculture at Oxford and, in the '30s, became one of the first organic farmers. During the Second World War he became Chairman of the Kent War Agricultural Committee and for 25 years he was Provost of Wye College—the agricultural college of London University. He was a passionate and inspired gardener and an artist.

At the same time, he sought a deeper meaning for his life, and conducted a long spiritual search. In mid-life, he found the answer he was looking for in the writings of the philosophers René Guénon and Frithjof Schuon, who were the founders of what later became known as the 'traditionalist' or 'perennialist' school.

He became increasingly concerned that modern scientific discoveries—important in their own domain—were being inappropriately used to discredit a more traditional and holistic understanding of the meaning of the Universe and of man's role in it. The collection of essays which form the chapters of this, his last book, reflect that concern and explore some of the ways in which the concept of linear evolutionary progress has influenced contemporary thinking. He restates some of the fundamental metaphysical truths which can be found, in one form or another, underlying the teaching of all the great Traditions and Religions of the World.

In this edition I have made alterations to punctuation and to the form of some sentences to enhance readability. I have also carried to a footnote some of the points which disturbed the flow of the argument. I believe and hope that these changes do not alter the meaning or integrity of the text.

Christopher James
5th Lord Northbourne

I
Introductory

Any intelligible conception of progress must be directional; that is to say, it must imply the simultaneous conception of a goal. When the conception of progress is applied to humanity as a whole, or to any section of it, the way in which that goal is conceived depends on the answers given to certain questions that are as old as mankind: questions such as 'What is the universe?' 'What is life?' 'What is man?'

The search for answers to such questions is nothing less than the unending search of humanity for a stable principle to which all experience can be referred. That search is being pursued in one way or another as intensively today as ever before. As always, the directions in which it is pursued are contingent on the tendencies of the prevailing mentality.

The purpose of this chapter is to draw attention to the contrast between two mentalities. One or the other is almost always predominant. They arrive at different answers to the kind of questions already mentioned, and they can conveniently be distinguished as 'traditional' and 'progressive'. In subsequent chapters that contrast will be amplified from various points of view.

The traditional mentality, in the sense in which the word is used here, is characteristic of societies in which a revealed religion, together with the accompanying tradition, exercises a predominant influence. The progressive mentality is one in which a science founded on observation, together with a humanistic philosophy based on that science, is the mainspring of thought and action. Only within the last few centuries has the latter mentality become predominant. Almost everyone would agree that a profound change of outlook has taken place during that period, and that it first became predominant in Western Europe, from whence it has spread to the rest of the world.

This change is commonly regarded as being of the nature of an awakening to reality, or as an opening up of new horizons, or as a development of powers previously latent, and in any case as representing a progress leading from a state of relative ignorance and subservience to one of relative awareness and freedom.

The present confused and unhappy state of the world proves that the hoped-for results of this change of outlook have not yet been realized. Nevertheless, the world seems to see no hope of their realization except by way of an intensification and acceleration of the intellectual, social and economic developments consequent on this change. Is it not time to question the validity of the direction of our present aims, rather than thinking only about our efficiency in pursuing them?

The fact that the unending search of humanity is essentially a search for freedom from the constraints that seem to be inseparable from terrestrial life proves that we are conscious that our terrestrial situation is in a real sense a bondage. Less often are we fully conscious of the dual nature of that bondage. For we are bound in the first place by the constraints imposed on us by our environment, that is to say, by everyone and everything that is other than ourselves; this is our outward situation, the 'destiny we meet'. We are bound also to our own individual physical and mental heritage, which we did not choose for ourselves; this is our *ego*, our inward situation, the 'destiny we are'. The fact that we can be aware of our subjection to this double bondage, and can see it as such, is proof (if proof were needed) that our whole being is more than its terrestrial manifestation. We are strangers here, and we know it, even when we behave as though the place belonged to us and as if we were answerable to nothing and nobody but ourselves.

We are always more or less consciously trying to escape from some aspect of our double bondage. Two main lines of action are possible, related respectively to the two sides of its dual nature. One is to try to free the ego from the constraints imposed on it by its environment, that is to say, to improve its outward situation. That is what most of us are trying to do for most of the time. The other is to try to escape from the limitations of the ego as such. In other words, we can aspire to freedom *for* our terrestrial nature, or we can aspire to freedom *from* our terrestrial nature.

The choice is not between two alternative and more or less equivalent options. If our main objective is to bring our environment into subjection so that it may not restrict the freedom of our ego, we are not even going half-way towards release from our double bondage. So long as we are not inwardly free, we cannot take advantage of whatever our environment may have to offer, even though it should be wholly under our command and at our disposal.

Progress achieved towards the satisfaction of terrestrial needs, desires and fancies contributes nothing by itself towards inward freedom; on the contrary, when pursued beyond what is necessary, it tends more and more to supplant and to suppress the search for inward freedom, thereby defeating its own ends. Yet it is precisely such a progress that has become almost the sole aim of contemporary humanity. Its goal is to possess or to command everything in its environment. This last sentence describes very simply the way we have chosen. It is the way of those who give first place to the freeing of the ego from outward constraints, and it is the natural choice of the mentality that has been summarily called 'progressive'.

It is less easy to describe the other way. That way is associated with the traditional mentality. Its final goal is not to command things external to itself, but rather to surpass itself. The knowledge that it seeks above all is not a knowledge of the outer world but a knowledge that will enable it to command itself, and this implies a knowledge of itself. It does not deny the validity nor the necessity of some command over and some knowledge of the outer world, but this must not supplant or suppress self-knowledge. Self-knowledge cannot come by observation. Observation implies a duality between observer and observed, knower and known. Nothing that can be observed is identifiable with the observer. Therein resides the whole difficulty. Despite its overriding importance it is one which a science based wholly on observation can only ignore.

If nothing that we can possibly know distinctively is that within us which knows (either in sensorial or in cognitive mode) then our bodies and our souls (to the extent that they can be objects of distinctive knowledge) are external or peripheral with respect to our inmost being, to the 'self that knows'. This proves, if proof were needed, that they are not 'ourselves'. Yet paradoxically, our inmost being is really the only thing we do know for sure, though our knowledge of it is non-distinctive and intuitive. It alone is our one absolute certainty. We can be in doubt and in dispute about outward things and their relationships, but not about our own existence, without which there would be no perception, no knowledge, no doubt and no dispute. Yet, although our intuitive awareness of it is the very starting-point of all our awareness, we cannot say what constitutes our own reality. As soon as we try to distinguish it, we are mentally trying to situate it outside itself so that it may examine itself, which is absurd, and is made even more so by the fact that it is essentially single and not multiple. Consequently, anything that we succeed in distinguishing is not the object of our search.

Thus we are faced with the apparent paradox of an inward reality and unity which we cannot observe, although we are aware of it more surely than we are of anything. We know moreover that everyone else is in the same position, so we must have a word for it. It can only be a token word, a name and not a description; and no word is more applicable than the word 'spirit'. That word derives from the Latin *spiritus*, meaning 'wind' or 'breath'. The ubiquitous and vivifying air, invisible in itself, but perceptible through its dynamic functions as wind or breath, is an adequate or natural symbol on the material plane of the unseizable principle of our being that we call 'spirit'.[1]

Human individuals differ one from another in the degrees of development of their faculties, but the existence of any one individual is not different in kind from the existence of any other; all are animated by the same principle of being. When we want to emphasize the transcendence of that principle with respect to ourselves or

---

1. The characteristics of an adequate or natural symbol are analogous on their own plane to those of a prototype on a higher plane, the symbol being necessarily on the plane of the observable and communicable. Our senses are adapted only to two planes of existence, the physical and the psychic. To suggest that these two planes comprise all possibility is to make our senses the measure of all things which, in view of their obvious limitations, is childish.

to the universe, or to emphasize its intrinsic uniqueness, we usually refer to it as 'the Spirit' with a capital S; but we also use the word without a capital, and sometimes in the plural, to express all sorts of different and more limited ideas. Such usages can give rise to confusion; nevertheless they can also serve to remind the discerning of the immanence, the ubiquity and (if the word be allowable) the 'non-specificity' of the Spirit itself. Our passion for exact definition, when it is indulged to excess, hides from us much that is precious, and even that which is most precious of all.

The Spirit is that of which the world and we ourselves are manifestations. Manifestation is an exteriorization or a deployment, implying change and movement in an outward direction; correspondingly, the Spirit, the changeless and motionless Origin, is inward with respect to its manifestations, including ourselves. Although it is not strictly speaking localizable, we must look inward in order to find it.

We are often told that the objective of the 'way' we have collectively chosen, the outward-looking way, is to free the human spirit from bondage. If that is true, we are certainly going the wrong way about it. Our main endeavors are directed to the feeding—one might say to the fattening—of the desiring soul; of that aspect of the soul which is indissolubly attached to the body during life, and is the tightest of all the bonds that constrain the spirit, and the most difficult to identify and to loosen.

The way which we have rejected, the inward-looking way, seeks to free the human spirit from all its bonds by freeing it from those that are internal in the sense that they are part of the *ego*. It is they that confine the spirit most closely. In its purest form, this way is the way of the saint, whose goal is the unseizable Spirit and whose inward state it is beyond the power of words to convey.[2] But everyone cannot be a saint, so this same way is by extension the collective way of

---

2. Therefore anyone who tries to convey the nature of that inward state in words necessarily fails. This may not matter when both speaker and hearer are aware of the inadequacy of words in this connection; but when the inevitable failure is hidden in a morass of psychological jargon, which convinces many people by its apparent profundity that it has penetrated to the depths, then it matters very much indeed.

all communities whose traditions, laws, customs and habitual outlook are predominantly directed towards the pursuit of sanctity, and therefore towards the support of the saint as its vehicle, either directly through religious rites and observances and the selection and training of individuals, or indirectly through the maintenance and defense of a political, economic and social order so directed that the main aim can be effectively pursued within it.

This kind of indirect support is normally the principal function of a large majority. By its exercise the participation of everyone in the pursuit of sanctity is made possible, whatever his situation or capacity. Such, in principle, is the framework of a traditional civilization, although it is of course never perfectly realized. Such a society is never immune from degeneration and abuse, as we can see all too clearly today everywhere.

All civilizations were originally traditional in outlook; each one has attributed its own origin to an initial divine revelation or inspiration, and has regarded itself as the appointed preserver and guardian of the content of that revelation.

This generalization is valid despite great differences in the outward forms of traditional civilizations, despite their many and obvious imperfections, and despite their impermanence. Their differences manifest the fact that the Spirit cannot be confined by any specific form. It can however manifest itself fully in an indefinity

---

The withdrawal of the saint from the world, in his search for that which is within himself, is sometimes criticized as being selfish, on the grounds that he does not appear to be doing what he might do for the good of other people. The truth is the exact opposite. He is seeking a truth that can only be found by inner experience and not by observation, and it is the very truth without which humanity is lost. He is not seeking to obtain anything to satisfy his selfish ego, on the contrary, he is seeking to give himself wholly to God in love, and thereby to learn what love really is. The repercussions of his intense activity, which is undertaken on behalf of humanity, are unpredictable, and they are independent of whether he is a public figure or totally unknown to his fellow men. The inward experience of the saint brings a supra-rational certitude, whereas observation brings no more than probability, which is not the same as certitude, even when it is of a very high order. The modern world is conscious of many of its own deficiencies; it does not appear to be at all troubled about its lack of saints, although that is the deficiency that matters most of all and cannot be compensated for by anything else.

of different forms, sometimes mutually incompatible, without betraying itself, and always revealing itself. Their impermanence is a simple consequence of the fact that no civilization has ever been perfect, since it is a human and a temporal phenomenon; it is a manifestation of the Spirit, but it is not the Spirit itself which alone is imperishable. Everything, save the Spirit itself, carries within itself the seeds of its own dissolution.

Anyone who is disposed to emphasize the defects of traditional civilizations would do well to look dispassionately at our modern progressive—and therefore anti-traditional—civilization, and to look at it as it is, and not at what he thinks it is meant to be, or could be if only we could overcome this or that problem, or if only so-and-so would see sense. He should look at what it has in fact produced in the way of contentment, peace, beauty or freedom, and then at what it has in fact produced in the way of anxiety, war and rivalry, ugliness (in the despoiling of Nature and in the arts), and subjection to its own insatiable desires and to the inexhaustible demands of the machine. Then he should consider, no less dispassionately, what its prospects of durability appear to be, bearing in mind that all its present tendencies are bound to be accentuated in the future, their accentuation being in fact its principal objective. More and more and faster and faster is the cry, as if the end of a continuous quantitative expansion could be anything but dispersion and fragmentation, either gradual or explosive.

Some such questionings are at the back of many people's minds in one form or another today. Yet it seldom seems to occur to anyone to question the doctrine of progress in principle rather than merely in some of its consequences, nor yet to wonder seriously whether traditional civilizations may after all have possessed something we have lost, something that made life worth living even under conditions of poverty and hardship. Do we so excel in wisdom and virtue as to have the right to assume that they—our ancestors physically and intellectually—clung to tradition merely from stupidity, from a false sense of where their true interests lay, or from a superstitious blindness to the realities underlying their lives on earth? We are prepared to admit that they often produced sanctity and nobility in man and incomparable beauty in art, but we look down upon them for their submission to a traditional hierarchy, and for their acceptance of their often humble situations in it, and for their relative contentment with service to it. We think that they accepted these things because they knew no better, since they lacked a vision of the possibilities open to humanity. The question is, of course, whether it is the followers of tradition or the devotees of progress who are lacking in a vision of those possibilities.

If, as most people assume today, this life comprises all the possibilities open to humanity individually or collectively, then the satisfaction of the *ego*, the mitigation of pain and the postponement of death are indeed the best objectives we can choose, and we rightly accord first place to them. If, however, as the traditional view has it, death is a passage to another state of being in which we shall be confronted with the truth and see ourselves as we really are, and if pain is a reminder of the imperfection of our present state and as such not only inevitable but at least potentially beneficent, and if the salvation of the immortal soul takes precedence over the satisfaction of the ego, then the objectives named appear in a very different light. They do not become invalid, but to give them first place becomes both foolish and wicked. It seems to most people today to be foolish and even wicked to give them any other place. The attitudes and actions of traditional peoples seem to us often to be marked by both incomprehension and callousness. But what is the use of our achievements in mitigating pain and in postponing death if they are accompanied by the loss of the very thing that made life and death and pain both comprehensible and purposeful?

Tradition and hierarchy are inseparable. Together they constitute a chain linking civilization with the Spirit in successional mode and in simultaneous mode respectively; in time to a spiritual origin and in space to a spiritual center. The origin inspires the center, and the center perpetuates the origin.³ The whole structure is founded on the conception of the reality of divine revelation. Revelation alone confers on the chain of tradition its directional or centripetal force. Human beings are always to some extent mutually interdependent; they are always linked together by chains of various sorts, physical, economic, or ideological. But such chains are accidental; human desires may give them a direction, which is always centrifugal rather than centripetal. If the chain of tradition is anything at all, it is inherently directional and centripetal. It links mankind to its divine origin, and not to human wants or imaginings. Revealed religion is therefore the heart of tradition; without it tradition would be an empty shell, a form without significance; it would be no more than mere social convention. Conversely, tradition, with all its many manifestations that are not specifically religious in form, is the indispensable support of religion. Without that support religion cannot be integrated with life, it becomes a thing apart, a supplement rather than the principal directing force; it tends to degenerate into a vague individual belief in God, or into a mere ideology competing with other ideologies on their own plane.

---

3. The use of the word 'center' and cognate words in this connection is of course symbolical. The sphere is the type of all spatial forms and the most generalized. The center of a sphere is the point to which all its dimensions are referred; it defines the sphere regardless of its size or qualitative constitution. The center is dimensionless, but its influence pervades and coordinates the entire space; it is thus an adequate symbol of the dimensionless spiritual origin of all things, and that not only in a verbal sense, but also in the concrete form of the sacred locality, be it a temple, a holy city, a holy mountain, or the heart of man. For the spiritual center is in reality everywhere, and it is therefore unseizable. For that reason limited and localized beings who aspire towards it have need of a symbolical location to which they can direct their attention. And who can doubt that the Holy Spirit does indeed dwell in such places?

The fact that mankind feels the need of a symbolical center to which he can direct his aspirations makes possible, in periods of spiritual decadence, the substitution for the sacred center of other centers which are anything but sacred, but are simply rallying points for the delusions and passions of a humanity that has lost touch with a traditional center. They give rise to their own orders or systems which are often misleadingly referred to as hierarchies. The word 'hierarchy' comes from the Greek and means 'sacred order' and nothing else; it ought therefore to be applied only to a strictly traditional order, wherein all authority even in its social aspects, derives its legitimacy from the sacred center.

Religion and tradition are inseparable, they are two closely related aspects of the same thing. They are however seldom met with in their pristine purity, since their temporal manifestations necessarily carry within themselves the seeds of their own dissolution, as has already been indicated. Those seeds germinate slowly but, like weeds in a crop, once well established can overwhelm the crop and even virtually replace it altogether. The process is gradual but accelerative. At most times there is a mixture of crop and weed in varying proportions. The assessment of the exact proportion of each present at any given time may be difficult; but it is always possible to discern and to describe the intrinsic nature of each.

The point of departure of the traditional approach to reality is everywhere and always the same. This is true despite great differences in the historical development of traditional civilizations. Existence is envisaged as proceeding from an origin or prime cause which is transcendent with respect to all its productions, and is symbolically the center from which all existence radiates without ever becoming detached from it, on pain of ceasing to be. It is the center not only of the universe, the macrocosm, but also of the individual being, the microcosm, since the latter reflects the wholeness of the former.

In any community, its own particular sacred center, and in the individual, the heart, represents or symbolizes the universal center.[4] Therefore the gaze of the intelligent individual in search of the source of existence, or, what amounts to the same thing, the source

---

4. The psycho-physical complex that constitutes a human individual is a coherent unit, a little world on its own, a microcosm. All its organs are mutually interdependent, and each has a distinct function. Most people nowadays would regard the brain as performing the highest function of all, but the function of the brain, and the nervous system that is continuous with it, is mainly one of interpretation and co-ordination. It is the heart, and not the brain, that vivifies the whole, and is therefore the source of all its Potentialities, including the potentiality of intelligence. The correspondence on their respective planes between the heart and the spiritual center is therefore far from being merely fanciful. (See also note 3). When the heart is spiritually inert, the individual is not truly alive, but is a mere machine, however active the mind or the body may be. When the heart is spiritually active, the individual is truly alive, and is at peace whether he be outwardly active or not. 'I sleep, but my heart waketh' (Song of Songs 5:2).

of truth, is directed inwards, towards the sacred center of his particular world, and at the same time towards the center of his own being. His outlook on all that he sees and knows is conditioned by the direction of his aspiration. In more familiar words, he 'seeks the Kingdom of Heaven where it is to be found,' namely, 'within you'. It is worth noting that the word 'you' (or *vos* in Latin) can equally well be taken to be addressed to the collectivity with its more or less localized sacred center, or to the individual with his heart. Wherever tradition is the controlling principle of human activity, every man, whether he be intelligent or not, and whatever his function, is (consciously or otherwise) involved in this centripetal tendency.

The point of departure of the progressive outlook on reality, closely associated as it is with modern science, is observation. It looks exclusively outwards towards its environment, and not inwards towards the principle of its own being, which is at the same time the principle of all being. It does not consider existence as such, but only things that exist, and it regards their forms and qualities as products of their observable structure and their interaction with each other. It seeks to discern and to define the modes of operation of these interactions, hoping to discover some kind of fundamental law governing all relationships, and thus to arrive at something which, if not the absolutely prime cause of all things, represents at least as near an approach thereto as can be made by the human mind. Its point of departure precludes its taking into account anything which is not within the capacity of the human mind. God, therefore, must either be rejected or be rationalized and humanized, and the consequence is that religion is eventually reduced to the status of an unproved hypothesis, 'improbable' first in the etymological and then in the contemporary sense of the word. Thence it is but a step to the total rejection of religion, or to its substitution by ideologies or fancies originating exclusively in the brain or the sentiments of men. Tradition dies. Man is in no doubt about his own reality, and thus becomes supreme in his own eyes. At this point it becomes possible to say that man is now god.[5]

---

5. These very words constitute as it were the text of the Reith lectures on the B.B.C. for 1967, given by Prof. R. MacLean. But he is not the first to make a public

Nothing then remains but to glorify as far as possible man's achievements in subordinating his environment to his desires, a difficult task, in view not only of the triviality of those achievements on a terrestrial, and still more on a cosmic, scale, but above all in view of their conspicuous failure to satisfy. However, such talk is eagerly swallowed by a public acutely anxious about its own future, and all too ready to escape from facts into the realm of anticipations and to delude itself by considering, not what is, but what could be, if only science could have its way.

The outward look is separative. It emphasizes the duality between observer and observed, knower and known, man and Nature. Our environment becomes something to be exploited, albeit 'sustainably'. We become more conscious of it as an obstacle to the fulfillment of our desires than of our oneness with it. And since our human neighbor is, for each one of us, part of his environment, men become more and more separated one from another. The separativity of the outward look, when it is not balanced by its inward counterpart, divides man from his neighbor as well as from God, so that there is no longer a human family with God as its 'Father' and Nature as its 'Mother'. Reality itself is departmentalized; it tends to disintegrate, and man becomes ever more lonely and puzzled.

By contrast, the inward look is unitive. The seeker who finds the center, the knower who knows himself, sees both himself and the outside world, Nature and his neighbor, as one through their connection with that center, not through their chance linkages with each other. Unity becomes the reality, separativity and relativity the illusion. Powerful though that illusion be, yet for him it is so to speak transparent. Yet he knows that he as an individual does not occupy a situation fundamentally different from that of his neighbor. Unity, which is indivisible, cannot therefore appertain to him alone. If he is sane, he knows that he as an individual is not God; or

---

statement to this effect. Some years ago a pronouncement stating that 'the people are now god' came from Soviet Russia, certainly without official disapproval. In the Russian case it appeared that man was considered to be qualified for a divine status by his merits rather than by his capacities. whereas in Prof. MacLean's case the main qualification appears to be ingenuity.

alternatively, that if he can in any legitimate sense be said to be one with God, the same can be said of his neighbor. He knows that his own separate existence is in the last analysis both illusory and paradoxical; but this knowledge is all a part of his overriding certitude that God is, and alone is wholly real, and that Nature, his neighbor and himself, distinct though they be and even often in conflict, are one in God, and in God alone.

If the traditional view is the right one, the idea that progress, in the modern sense of the word, could ever fulfill the hopes and plans of its advocates must be deceptive, not primarily because men are weak, stupid, passionate and sometimes vicious, nor yet because human desires are so often mutually incompatible, but primarily because the advocates of a scientific and progressive humanism are looking away from the luminous source of their being, which is reflected in the divine spark in their own hearts. They are looking towards a universe which, in the absence of a valid principle, appears to be made up of particles and blind forces in ceaseless conflict with the desires and delusions of the human ego. Accordingly, they inflate and even deify the human ego in order to convince it that victory is possible. The voice of a progressive humanism proclaims that man has at last found the means of satisfying his desires, thus opening up the possibility of his becoming the creator of an earthly paradise. He can at last see his way to getting all he wants from his environment, provided that he will work hard and be reasonable. The voice of tradition on the other hand, when it is not enfeebled or afraid to speak out, proclaims that the worth, the dignity, the whole justification of human life lies in the preservation of the chain that binds man to God, who is his origin, preserver and end, whose Paradise is the only Paradise; and further, that in order to find that Paradise man must seek it in the sacred center, and not in the periphery.

The measure of our bondage is the strength of our attachment to the world of our experience and the extent of our submission to the desires engendered by that attachment. We deceive ourselves if we seek to escape from our bondage by way of the satisfaction of those desires. The measure of our deception is the extent of our failure to realize that those desires, being fed to excess, will multiply and plague us the more. Instead, we can seek to forestall and counteract too strong an attachment to the world by giving priority to a conscious and active aspiration towards the eternal Principle of our being which, being changeless, is above and beyond all attachment and all desire.

We have the freedom to choose which of these two attitudes or tendencies shall predominate and which shall be subordinate in directing the course of our lives. Collectively we have chosen, and must accept the consequences, but the individual is always free to conform to that collective choice or to reject it. If he rejects it, he can act only within the limits of the possibilities of his individuality and his situation. God does not ask the impossible of anyone. Tradition and all it implies being virtually a dead letter, he will get little help from his environment and much hindrance. He will have to face not only open hostility, but also much more subtle and often tempting subversive influences, which are of many different kinds and have invaded every domain, even the very domain of religion itself.

It may be thought that compromise of some kind must be possible, but the situation is such that compromise can never be anything but superficial and illusory. The opposition between the traditional and the progressive outlooks is strictly analogous to that between East and West, upward and downward, inward and outward, or any other two diametrically opposed directions. Since life is all movement and change, necessitating choice at every turn, an inward choice between the two directions is inescapable, even though it may seem to be involuntary or unconscious. That choice, and it alone, determines the orientation of the soul and therewith its fate. At the same time it determines the ultimate effect of every act.

In these days when circumstances seem to impose compromise, it is no small thing to assert the impossibility of an effective compromise between the two ways of approach to truth here designated as traditional and progressive. Individuals and societies frequently attempt compromises between things that are in reality incompatible, but when that is the case any apparent compromise is illusory and cannot endure. One or the other of the two factors involved is bound to win in the end. This generalization applies fully to the present case, and it is not difficult to see which of the two approaches in question appears now to be winning. The question is whether its final victory is possible. If it is impossible that the approach of modern science should penetrate to the foundations of the reality of existence, simply because that science is looking in the wrong direction, then the fact that tradition is disappearing and religion seems to be in eclipse does not affect in the slightest degree the certainty of the final victory of the approach that leads to truth, although the form that victory will take cannot be predicted.

Before concluding this introductory chapter, three further points must be made. In the first place, it is often suggested that either modern psychology, or a philosophy that has developed in parallel with modern science, is working in the same direction as that pursued by traditional sages and philosophers and by the few who still seek to follow them, and that it is thus making an approach to the same goal. That is not so. The approach of modern psychology and philosophy coincides consciously and deliberately with that of modern science. It is a search for an outward and distinctive knowledge, either in order to gain more control over the environment or ourselves, or with no avowed objective other than that of increasing the sum of human knowledge. In either case, what is involved is the exteriorization and examination of phenomena with as much scientific detachment as possible. The word detachment is very significant, because it implies the most complete separation possible between subject and object, knower and known. Such is the way of science. It has its own validity and produces its own kind of results; its dispassion is exemplary; nevertheless, the direction of its approach is diametrically opposed to that of what has, so far very briefly, been described as the traditional way. It therefore cannot lead to the same goal.[6]

---

6. If this is true in principle, nevertheless its application to particular cases is often difficult. In the case of psychology, the difficulty resides in the fact that, in its investigation of the 'sub-conscious', it often fails to distinguish between the 'supra-conscious', and the 'infra-conscious', that is to say, between what is too exalted to

The second point is more fundamental. There is an apparent illogicality in saying that the nature, or the end-point, of what one is talking about cannot be specified in words, and then going on talking about it. Might it not be better to retire within oneself and be silent? Well, it might. To do so would at least avoid the risk of leaving the reader puzzled or angry or, worse, bored. It is a serious risk. The reasons for taking that risk could be stated in many ways, among others as follows.

Words are primarily evocative; their descriptive use is conditional on their evocative power. They convey no meaning at all unless they fall into correspondence with some potentiality present or latent in the hearer. Only then do they evoke a response of any kind. The possibility of their descriptive use depends on their evocative power, but description is restricted to the plane of our terrestrial life. Words are in any case all derived from our common experience on that plane. If that plane alone comprises the whole of reality there is no further argument; but, if there are other planes of reality, they too are accessible to the purely evocative potentiality of words by virtue of the analogical relationship subsisting between all planes, and constituting the basis of all true symbolism.[7] Those who would limit the use and understanding of words to their purely descriptive function are, among other things, reducing to the commonplace all the Sacred Scriptures, and all the great poetry, writings and sayings that have ever pierced the veil of the terrestrial involvement of mankind. Let us admit once and for all that this world is no better than commonplace unless it is lifted out of itself towards a plane higher than its own. By the Grace of God it can be, provided that we do not

---

descend into the distinctive consciousness and what is too debased to be raised to that level. It might be thought that such a distinction must be self-evident; but a right discrimination between the two is not within the power of the mind, because the 'sub-conscious' is by definition excluded from the conscious mind; it can therefore only be accomplished by way of an interior or spiritual vision. Where that vision is lacking, either accidentally or because an approach that excludes it is adopted on principle, the result is a fatal confusion. The approach of much contemporary philosophy excludes that vision on principle; it is therefore liable to lead to error, however plausible its arguments may seem to be on the purely mental plane.

7. See note 1, p4.

insist on limiting our understanding of symbols, verbal symbols included, to that of their most outward or 'literal' significance.

Finally: some people say that there is a conflict between religion and science, others say that there is not. Who is right? The two incompatibles, which for the sake of brevity have been labeled 'tradition' and 'progress', are not identifiable with religion and with science respectively, in the first place because there is and always has been a sacred science. Sacred science is not restricted in its outlook as modern science is. It sees the temporal universe of phenomena as no more than an appearance, and it seeks a supra-phenomenal and intemporal reality, just as religion does, but it follows a path which is parallel to, rather than coincident with, the path of religion, at least until both attain to the summit.

In the second place, a religion founded on revelation remains now as always indissolubly linked with tradition, and now as always it is centered on the supra-phenomenal and intemporal, even when, as a result of human weakness, it is not as evidently so as it might be. Meanwhile, science in its modern form has lost sight of the supra-phenomenal and intemporal, and has taken on the role of prophet, guide and provider to an ideology of progress having as its goal a temporal and terrestrial utopia.

There is a conflict, but it is not between religion and science as such, for they can be regarded as two normal, necessary and parallel approaches to truth, provided always that the hierarchical superiority of the religious approach is recognized and acted upon. The conflict is between the two points of view here designated respectively as traditional and progressive. Religion and science come into conflict only insofar as they are associated with the one or with the other.

Attempts at compromise between the traditional and progressive points of view, as applied to the origin and destiny of man and of the universe, can only lead to confusion. Their mutual incompatibility is total and unequivocal. The ideology of progress envisages the perfectibility of man in terms of his terrestrial development, and relegates it to a hypothetical future, whereas tradition envisages the perfectibility of man in terms of salvation or sanctification, and proclaims that it is realizable here and now.

II

Pictures of the Universe

There exists in the mind of every individual something that can be called a picture of the universe. It is an image built up, more or less consciously, from all that appears to that individual to constitute the reality or the relevance of the world of experience. Whether it be consciously realized or not, whether it be clear and coherent or very much the reverse, it provides a constant background to all his discursive thought and belief.

Throughout life the individual is constantly receiving impressions through his senses and encountering ideas communicated to him by other individuals. These experiences are interpreted according to his inborn constitution, physical, psychic and intellectual. In this way a picture gradually takes shape in his mind. This picture can differ very widely from one individual to another.

Generally speaking, in ancient civilizations the prevalent interpretations did not differ widely, because the validity of the common sensory experience was not questioned, and the ideas that give it meaning were more or less firmly established and fixed by tradition. Such a civilization has a distinctive character and some degree of integration and stability.

More recently, and particularly in Europe from the end of the Middle Ages onwards, the traditional fixity of intellectual and religious ideas has become gradually loosened. In modern times this tendency has become ever more rapidly accentuated, concurrently with the growth of the 'progressive' outlook. The results of scientific enquiry have caused the validity of the direct experience of the senses to be questioned for the first time in history. This questioning has in turn reacted on the intellectual and religious environment. The result is that modern civilization suffers from a dreadful confusion about what the universe really is, what is real and what is not, what to believe and what not to believe. For this reason it seems desirable to enquire into the intellectual standing of modern scientific discoveries.

The novelty of modern scientific discoveries and their effectiveness in application have suggested to many people that the universe is not what it had hitherto been supposed to be, and that therefore many of the intellectual and religious ideas prevalent in the past must be modified or superseded. The scientific outlook is as much a consequence as a cause of a more generalized tendency which can broadly and briefly be described as anti-traditional. Although modern science manifests this tendency very fully it is by no means alone in doing so.

The picture of the physical universe which modern science invites us to accept seems indeed to be very different from the picture suggested by the direct experience of the senses. For convenience, the first may be called the scientific picture and the second the natural picture. For example the scientific picture tells us that the apparent rising and setting of the sun is really only a subjective effect produced in us by the rotation of the earth; or that the apparent solidity and continuity of matter is a similar effect attributable to the extreme rapidity of the motion of certain widely spaced infinitesimal particles, or again that the experience of color is the subjective effect of wavelike vibrations occurring in an invisible, omnipresent and undifferentiated substratum. In each case the more complex and less self-evident picture is represented as being more realistic or more objective than the other, and less colored or distorted by the individual peculiarities of the observer. It is represented as being nearer to the truth, or nearer to some underlying reality, so that it in some way explains the natural picture, and reveals, or is on the way towards revealing, the causes underlying the common phenomena of experience, and with them the constitution and origins of the physical universe itself and all that it comprises, including man.

Insofar as the two pictures of the physical universe are mental constructions derived from sense perception they are not different in kind; the extent to which the senses may be aided by mechanical devices does not affect their validity in principle. The process of their formation is the same in both cases: it is a process of mental elaboration applied to data supplied through the senses. Therefore, if the natural picture is a delusion, so is the scientific. The only question can be whether the one is more so than the other. Similarly, if the natural picture is subjective, so is the scientific, and here again it can only be a question of degree.[1]

The scientific picture does not in fact replace the natural picture, but rather supplements and elaborates it. It can be separated from and contrasted with the natural picture, but there is no real discontinuity between the two. Elaboration alone does not necessarily contribute to objectivity. In this case elaboration might even be held to detract from objectivity, the commonly accepted test of objectivity being the coincidence of the impressions of normally constituted people. By that test the natural picture would appear as the more objective of the two, since it is common to all humanity. The scientific picture on the other hand is accessible in its authentic form only to a few mathematicians. In its popularized forms, wherein, for instance, the elementary particles are pictured as if they partook of the nature of solid matter, it is greatly simplified and inevitably distorted in order to bring it within the range of the non-specialist.

The natural picture remains what it always was: the sun rises and sets, rocks stand firm, the lightning strikes, the sky is as blue and blood is as red as they ever were. The scientific picture becomes ever more remote and strange. For instance, the infinitesimal 'particles' mentioned above comprising electrons, protons and many others, in no way resemble material particles. They have been described as being more like systems of waves, and those waves have even been described as 'waves of thought' (Schrödinger), or as 'waves of probability' (Heisenberg). These 'particles' are in fact purely mathematical abstractions, elaborated by the human mind, and therefore no less characteristic of it and colored by its tendencies than any other

---

1. In this book the word 'objective' is used in its ordinary sense, as meaning 'existing independently of any observer,' and the word 'subjective', as its correlative, meaning 'originating exclusively in the observer.'

conception derived, directly or indirectly, from the experience of the senses.[2]

Any scientist of repute would agree that the scientific picture is eminently unstable and is continually developing. Its popularization lags ever farther behind its elaboration in the minds of scientific specialists. Nobody would suggest that the universe itself is constantly changing its nature; consequently an ever-changing representation of it must be provisional and cannot be truly objective.[3]

It is undeniable that a great many scientific conceptions have become more or less stabilized and popularized in the course of a relatively short period. Some appear to have come to stay, and to have provided a foundation for further developments, but those later developments have succeeded one another with ever increasing speed, and each one has brought about some change in the conception of what constitutes ultimate reality. Who can say what the next development will be, or how soon it will appear? Modern methods of electronically aided teamwork in research could, and probably will, accelerate the appearance of new developments to an extent hitherto unforeseen. The question is whether this situation is compatible with an increasing objectivity in the representation of what are supposed to be the most fundamental realities. Despite the fact that all these new ideas are products of the human mind, and that instability is far more characteristic of the human mind than of the universe it seeks to understand, there are many people who would answer that question in the affirmative, on the grounds that we are witnessing an important period in the progressive evolution of the human mind from a 'Primitive' to an 'advanced' state.

This notion is a facet of the much more general notion of progressive evolution, now so widely accepted as to have become almost axiomatic. It is regarded by most people, including scientists,

---

2. On the above grounds alone the superior objectivity of the scientific picture could well be questioned, even if it were more stable than it is in fact.

3. The natural picture on the other hand is at least relatively stable, whatever else it may be. Against this, it would be argued that no scientist of repute would claim that the scientific picture is complete, but that, on the contrary, the aim of science is to build up a picture of increasing objectivity, and that much progress has already been made in that direction, although much still remains to be done.

as a 'law of nature'. Its origins really lie in an attempt to formulate a purely physical explanation for the existence of a great diversity of species of animals and plants, all more or less well adapted to their environment.

The original Darwinian postulate, on which all subsequent variations are based, was that there are, in every species, variations as between one individual and another, which may be either frequent but so slight as to be barely perceptible, or rarer but more marked. In the latter case they are called 'mutations'. Harmful variations naturally tend to die out, beneficial ones to survive; thus in time individuals appear which are so different from their predecessors as to constitute new species.

There are many later versions of this hypothesis, differing mainly in their emphasis on the relative importance of the parts played by mutation and by natural selection respectively; their common factor is the postulate that the characteristics which distinguish one species from another are brought about by a more or less gradual process of 'evolution,' of which the effective causes, whether internal or external, are situated on the plane of physical existence rather than involving any more or less abrupt 'creation' of those characteristics by an effective cause situated elsewhere than on that plane. There are many questions which remain unanswered in relation to evolutionary theory.

Any version of the evolutionary hypothesis postulating a continuity between one species and another must find a way of setting aside the paleontological evidence,[4] which indicates that a very long time ago—on the terrestrial time-scale but not on the cosmic—there were few or no living creatures on the earth. Pre-Cambrian fossils are unknown, Cambrian are very few. In all later periods the earth was fully populated, each geological epoch having a characteristic fauna and flora, composed of many species, some of them highly developed. This state of affairs seems to have arisen with remarkable suddenness. Each species appears abruptly in a recognizable and

---

4. For a full discussion of this aspect of the matter, and of others as well, the reader is referred to *The Transformist Illusion*, by Douglas Dewar (Ghent, NY: Sophia Perennis, 1995).

stable form, and remains so until it dies out. There are however instances of a series of species which appears to lead step by step towards a final form; the horse is an 'example; but in all such cases the steps are well marked, each one is so distinct from its neighbors as to have been accorded specific rank, and there are no intermediate graduations.

The evidence supplied by the contemporary scene is also relevant. Are not most of the characteristics of living creatures as it were gratuitous, even when not actually disadvantageous? If the cause underlying their infinitely varied forms were purely, so to speak, utilitarian (and this is a basic assumption of the evolutionary hypothesis) would the world be anything like what it is today? Would it not be as dull and uniform as the utilitarian monstrosities with which we are now engaged in disfiguring the face of nature? The differences in shape, color and texture of leaves alone make nonsense of any hypothesis in which natural selection plays a major part.[5] Natural selection no doubt has a part to play, though it is probably a purely negative one; but some other factor is predominant. To call that other factor 'chance' is merely to admit an ignorance of causes; to call it a 'vital urge' or a 'tendency to diversification' or anything of the kind is merely an attempt to cover up ignorance by giving it a name.

It is very difficult to see why, if individual species or characteristics are products of a gradual evolution, any distinct or definable species are discoverable at all, or ever have been. Why is there not an indefinite series of forms all merging into one another? If the notion of evolution does not imply a gradual development of species and characteristics, how does it differ from a 'creationist' conception? How is it that habits and characteristics of many creatures are of such complexity that it is impossible to imagine how they can have arisen step by step, since one step is nothing without the others, and the failure of one is the failure of the whole?

Another question that needs to be satisfactorily answered concerns beauty. How is it that so many living creatures manifest beauty

---

5. The author was a botanist and plantsman as well as an experienced gardener. ED.

in some degree or in some kind? Beauty is sometimes 'explained' as an important factor in sexual attraction, and therefore in natural selection; but in an overwhelming majority of cases its occurrence can have no relation to any such function. Beauty appears also sometimes to be regarded as a purely 'subjective' phenomenon, with the implication that it has no particular importance, or as a mere 'accident' or even 'luxury', and in any case as being unrelated to the serious business of life. Any such attempt to minimize the significance of beauty is not only an expression of pure quantitative materialism, but also a denial of some of the most positive and some of the most precious of human experiences.

The systems of modern science are based on certain kinds of human experience—for example the experiences of weight or of light or of heat—which it can relate to measurable or numerable factors; the experience of beauty and other purely qualitative experiences elude all attempts at reduction to calculable factors; they are therefore by definition beyond the range of modern science. The scientific point of view is often reluctant to admit that anything of importance is beyond its range, and so things that do not fit neatly into its systems are ignored or explained away. The traditional point of view admits straight away that beauty is a more or less direct reflection of a divine attribute; a gift of God.

The evolutionary hypothesis is based on the idea of adaptation to environment. It is pertinent to ask how it is that the epithet 'progressive' has come to be attached to it so often. There does not seem to be any suggestion that the many changes in the environment that have taken place in the past were themselves 'progressive' in any recognizable sense of the word, so why should adaptation to them constitute a 'progress'? 'Regress' is just as probable; and it seems in fact to be no less frequent. If there is anything that can be called an evolution, there is also an involution. Thus, even if the scientific hypothesis could be accepted in other respects, there can be no justification for describing evolution as 'progressive'; the reasons for its being so described are in fact purely sentimental and 'wishful'.

There also seems to be today a very strange and prevalent confusion between two totally different conceptions of progress, namely, that associated with the evolutionary hypothesis in its scientific form, and that associated with a political or social ideal of progress. The former envisages only changes in the constitution of living beings; the latter envisages changes in the environment of those beings, and it apparently assumes that such changes will tend towards the development of a superior type. Since acquired characters are not inherited, there appear to be no grounds for any such assumption. On the contrary, if any kind of natural selection or adaptation to environment are indeed important factors in the progressive evolution of living creatures, then surely a harsh and demanding environment would be more conducive to progress than a soft and undemanding one, and inversely. This of course is no new idea. It has been held and put into practice in the past by individuals and collectivities in various ways, but it is unfashionable today.

There are realities that are expressible, and therefore at least in principle explicable, and there are realities that are neither expressible nor explicable. The latter comprehend the former.

No attempt to account for the forms of living creatures, and *a fortiori* for their existence, by reference to expressible realities alone can possibly succeed. That is not to say however that it is impossible to deduce any kind of comprehensible and comprehensive law from a study of the universe in all its observable aspects. If the universe has a cause, as it must, that cause cannot but be manifested in it.

Without attempting to deal fully with that aspect of the matter, it may be suggested that one such law is clearly discernible. It could be described as a law of formation, duration and dissolution; or by analogy with living things, as a law of birth, life and death. It is applicable to all systems, from man to amoeba, and from spiral nebula to the atom. It is applicable not only to man himself as an individual, but also to every human institution and achievement, and to every possible distinctive mental conception, from the most evanescent of dreams to the great religions and philosophies themselves; and therefore, inevitably, to modern science in all its aspects and productions, and with all its hypotheses, the evolutionary included.

The law of birth, life, and death does not justify an attitude of despair. Every positive quality subsists eternally in principle, whether it be manifested or not. Everything that has form manifests in some degree some positive quality; if it did not do so it would be detached from its eternal principle and thus be deprived of all that makes it what it is, in other words, it would not exist. At the same time it denies other positive qualities, for if it did not do so it would not be distinguishable from its all-embracing principle. Everything is thus a mixture of positive and negative. The negative has no intrinsic reality; it is nothing without the positive that it denies, and thus it has no more than a contingent existence. When the negative disappears the mixture of positive and negative also disappears.

The world as we know it is just such a mixture. It is however the privilege and function of man to distinguish in all that he does between the positive and the negative, between truth and untruth, good and evil; and in making that distinction effective to play his part in bringing the world back towards the permanent and positive reality that gave it birth.

Let us return for a moment to the question of the standing of the evolutionary hypothesis in the world. It is strange that this hypothesis should be so assiduously maintained by scientists in the face of another scientific conception, long established and seldom if ever questioned. It is formulated in the second law of thermodynamics, the law of entropy, which describes the inevitable running down or dispersal of all concentrations of energy, however they may have originated. Life is more than energy alone, but without a factor of energy it would not be life on earth as we know it. Life as we know it cannot therefore claim exception from this law, and substitute a 'law' of progressive evolution. The two 'laws', the one describing an inevitable running down and the other an automatic progress, are mutually contradictory.

It is not at all strange that the 'law' of birth, life and death—which, like all other 'laws' of its kind is purely descriptive—should fit in very well with the traditional conception of the cyclical character of all terrestrial and celestial phenomena. That law has been formulated in many different ways in the various great religions and traditions. Peoples whose lives are regulated according to this conception never lose sight of the inevitability of an ending. The outlook of modern science, being confined to observable phenomena, can never envisage their end. Man cannot live without hope, so science supports the delusion of a progressive evolution operating within its own limited field of view.

Even if all that has just been said were admitted to be true, the changes brought about in the world around us by the application to industry of the modern scientific approach would still provide, in the minds of many people, an almost unanswerable argument in favor of the intellectual superiority of the scientific picture of the universe. Whatever may be the intellectual standing of the new ideas, it is impossible to deny that they produce results. Their effect on our daily lives is often described as revolutionary, and there is no need to quarrel with that description. How far does this fact indicate that the scientific picture is nearer to the truth than the other?

The mere falsity or otherwise of a notion is no measure of its power to produce results; activity misdirected is still activity, and as such it can lead to disaster. If anyone were to seek to show that modern science inevitably counterbalances its benefits by the release of uncontrollable destructive forces, he would be able to produce much evidence in support of that view, particularly if he took into account not only forces that can destroy the body, but also those that can destroy the soul, by depriving man of his humanity and enslaving him to the machine. Yet most people regard modern science as essentially beneficent. The common arguments rest not on truth and untruth, but on advantage and disadvantage, real or supposed, actual or potential; in other words, an emotive judgment is substituted for an intellectual one.

The advantages realized are confined exclusively to the increased availability of temporal satisfactions, physical, mental and emotional. Can the ability to procure temporal satisfactions properly be treated as an influential factor in the choice between truth and untruth, or between right and wrong? Certainly not; unless indeed all truth is relative and there is no absolute. If that were the position—and there are people who would maintain that it is so, and a vastly greater number who behave as if it were so—then indeed there is nothing to do but to eat, drink and be merry, relying on science to provide the means, while hoping that death is really a total extinction and not an awakening to reality.

But if ultimate truth is absolute and not relative, and if it can be approached otherwise than by reference to temporal welfare—then there is no justification for assuming that the power of modern science to produce results, even if they appear to be beneficent, is evidence of an intellectual superiority.[6]

The mere coexistence of two (or more) contrasting pictures of the universe has by itself produced much mental confusion and uncertainty. This confusion is greatly accentuated by the fact that the benefits arising from the advances of science seem in fact always to be counterbalanced by the development of new and terrifying possibilities.

If religion is founded on false assumptions, and if nothing else, not even solid matter, is really what it seems to be, and if anticipated benefits cannot be realized unaccompanied by a growing fear of the total destruction of the potential beneficiaries, where do we stand? Small wonder that confusion and fear interact and mutually reinforce one another. Clearly something is wrong, and the blame is usually assigned to human weakness or lack of goodwill or lack of education, so that only by intensifying our pursuit of observational knowledge, and by hastening its popularization and the application of its results, can we hope to get out of the mess. Only, that is to say, by a continuing acceleration of activity directed along the same lines as those which may reasonably be held to have played their part in creating the present confusion.

In our passionate desire to get something done we forget that the inexorability of the law of action and reaction has for long been established in physics, and that its application cannot be confined to that field alone. The two worlds, the physical and the psychic, do not exist independently one of the other. We behave as if the inevitable reaction could be escaped by ignoring it, and as if evolution did not imply a correlative involution.

---

6. In the past, and particularly in such periods as we may admit to have been marked by qualities of nobility or greatness, any such power would have been regarded with deep suspicion, as being all too probably the work of the devil.

We forget too that we can by no means place ourselves outside our human nature. The claim that the scientific picture provides a more reliable foundation for action because it is not colored, or at least is less colored than the other by the limitations of our human individuality, rests on the assumption that we can, deliberately and by taking thought, dissociate ourselves from that individuality and its limitations, and from our situation as constituent parts of the universe in order to examine it from a detached, uncolored, purely objective and indeed godlike point of view. The assumption has only to be stated in that form in order to stand out in all its inherent absurdity.

Since we are men and not gods, nothing but delusion can spring from our forgetting that we cannot detach ourselves from ourselves, and that our knowledge is part of ourselves. The visible universe, we ourselves and our knowledge are one; and all are perishable. Can truth possibly be served by our assumption of a godlike position which can never really be ours? Surely not. On the contrary: we would do better to try to realize and to accept the limitations of our present state; and to pay attention not only to its weakness, perversity and brutality, but also to the inescapable limitations of our powers of perception and of our understanding, while not forgetting that understanding is everything. If the understanding is weak or prejudiced, microscopes and telescopes only add quantitatively to the flow of information reaching us through the channel of the senses; they add nothing to the understanding of it, and the very weight and complexity of the information may even make its interpretation and synthesis more difficult rather than easier.

The quality of our awareness of our surroundings is conditioned by what we are, so is the effectiveness of any action motivated by that awareness. Our interpretation of the experience of our senses is conditioned by the quality of the 'light that is in' us. The quantitative aspect of our experience is of small importance; its variety and complexity are accidents and bear no relation to the quality of our interior vision. One man may travel far and wide and see only the outward appearance of things (and sometimes not much of that); another may live all his life in one place and by virtue of the quality of his interior vision 'see God in all things'. One man may form a highly complex and abstruse picture of the physical world—a picture not invalid in itself in its proper context—and yet be unable to penetrate its opacity; another may form a very simple picture, but one that is perfectly valid as far as it goes, and at the same time see it as if it were transparent, like a prism refracting the pure light beyond it. The highly elaborated picture, insofar as it is formed as a result of the acquisition and collation of a vast quantity of factual information, is relatively quantitative, and as such it tends to be more opaque than the other. What really matters is the interior vision of the observer, the 'light that is in' him. The quotation, it will be remembered, continues: 'and if that light be darkness, how great is that darkness!'

It is not so much what a man sees that matters, but how he sees it. In vain does he probe the recesses of the universe in both directions, from the unimaginably great to the unimaginably small, unless it leads him to a better knowledge of himself, to a firmer hold on his own soul. The vastness and complexity of the physical universe may encourage a sense of wonder and corresponding humility in some people in whom those potentialities are already present and only waiting to be awakened; but all too often it seems to have the opposite effect, namely that of encouraging an overweening pride, which shows itself in a sense of superiority over all peoples past and present who saw, or see, the universe more directly and more simply; more 'as a little child'. This pride effectively inhibits any recognition of the fact that the simpler view is not necessarily accompanied by a lesser understanding of what the universe really is, and of the fact that the said probings contribute very little to that kind of understanding, for they tell us only what the universe looks like to us when first subjected to a particular kind of analytical examination.

They do indeed provide an enormous quantity of information about the world of the senses, most of it physical and some of it psychological. The objectivity of much of this information need not be questioned; for example, certain measurements, such as the mean distances of the planets from the sun or the frequencies of many vibrations, can be regarded as established; but such objective information is something very different from the purely hypothetical notions which have come to be treated by the non-scientific public, and by some scientists as well, as if they ranked as objective information, for example the evolutionary hypothesis and certain abstruse atomic hypotheses.

The objective information available is insignificant in relation to all that remains unknown, as many scientists would admit. Nevertheless, it is all that modern science has to offer, and it is all comprised within the field of physical experience, to which everything, including psychological experience, is as far as possible reduced.

The modern scientific point of view rejects *a priori* all that can properly be called metaphysical, and therewith all that could provide a point of reference to which physical experience could be related. The consequence of trying to understand the physical in terms of the physical is inevitably a gyration in closed circles, leading eventually to error and contradiction. The contemporary philosophy of science is always trying to escape from this situation, but it is impossible that it should do so while it remains blind to the metaphysical, that is to say, while it retains its present foundations. The scientific vocabulary sometimes makes use of the word 'metaphysics', but only in connection with some purely mental construction designed to eliminate as far as possible the inexpressible; whereas the purpose of metaphysic in the rightful sense of the word is precisely to suggest as far as possible the inexpressible. Thus the same word comes to be applied to things that have contrary objectives. The scientific picture is well equipped to provide certain kinds of information, but it denies itself the possibility of interpreting that information; the amassing of more and more information brings it no nearer to being able to do so.[7]

---

7. But it can see no way out other than a continued extension of the range of physical experience, which is therefore pursued relentlessly, and dignified under the

Thus the picture of the universe presented by modern science becomes ever more complex and remote from the natural picture. Nevertheless, independently of any question as to its relative validity, it exists as an influential factor in contemporary thought; that being the case it is part of ourselves and part of the universe. Its ultimate cause cannot be other than the ultimate cause of all things, and like all other things, including the natural picture, the scientific picture can be seen as a symbol of its cause, that is to say, as a partial reflection of that cause on the plane of appearances. When its outward form alone is considered, that form becomes a more or less impenetrable veil, hiding the cause, but if its symbolical significance can be discerned, that form can reveal the cause. From this point of view the most important difference between the two pictures is that the symbolism of the natural picture is much more direct and much more evident than that of the other. Both are veils, but one is much less opaque than the other. Both are symbols, but one is much more easily seen as such than the other. Hence the constant reference to the natural picture in the Sacred Scriptures. Hence also the real importance to us of virgin nature. Fortunately, the natural picture is always with us, for it is nearer both to virgin nature and to our common nature, and both are near to God.

Many people may find it difficult to accept this statement as valid in some cases, for example when the natural picture represents the surface of the earth as flat and not spheroidal; but such a case is not necessarily excluded, provided that this conception is natural and that no sufficient reason for modifying it is immediately apparent. It does not apply when any such belief is maintained merely through obstinacy or affectation. Similarly in the case of many other interpretations of directly experienced natural phenomena which would in these days be dismissed as 'unscientific'. So far from being incompatible with a vision of the reality underlying the appearance, they may be at least as compatible with it as some more highly elaborated and more sophisticated picture.

---

name of 'research'. For these reasons also the philosophy in question must gloss over, distort, or deny religion, for religion is derived from metaphysical principles, even though they may for a time be more or less clouded over or forgotten.

We cannot escape from the world of appearances for so long as we ourselves are constituent parts of it, but an excessive attention to the details of its observable features may distract attention from the reality it reflects. It is not for us to despise or to refuse to accept the appearance, in whatever form it may present itself to us, but rather to see in it a symbol of a transcendent reality. There is therefore no reason to be ashamed of thinking that the direct experience is relevant, and for most people far more relevant, than the elaborated and indirect experience, whether it be a case of the rising and setting of the sun, the solidity of matter, the blueness of the sky, or even the relative flatness of the little bit of earth on which we stand. We shall therefore do well to recognize that people who know nothing but the natural picture are not necessarily farther from the truth than we are, and to be careful about adopting an attitude of superiority towards them.

Traditional wisdom in all its authentic forms, religious or otherwise, is concerned directly with the basic realities of which all appearances, including all valid pictures of the universe, are reflections on one plane or on another. It is not therefore directly concerned with the nature of any particular picture, but rather with its symbolical content. The symbolism of religion is based on the picture of the physical world which is common to all men, and not on the highly specialized and mentally elaborated picture presented by modern science, which is by no means common to all men.[8] But since the scientific picture comprises an element of truth, it must also have a symbolical content which can be discerned by those who have the necessary qualifications (but by them alone). There are records and monuments of extinct civilizations which indicate that some of the elements of the modern scientific picture of the physical universe,

---

8. The scientific picture in no way invalidates their common experience, but as it grows more abstruse is ever less immediately present to their consciousness. It may indeed be purely conceptual, in which case nobody can experience it directly.

particularly in the field of astronomy, must have been known in those days to an intellectual elite. They were not normally divulged to the majority; who were much better off without them—that is to say, with nothing but the evident symbolism of the direct picture, and without the complications arising from the necessity of reconciling the two, or of situating each in its proper place. That is precisely what we ourselves so conspicuously fail to do, thereby unconsciously justifying the policy of the wise men of old.

The religions make use of a symbolical language simply because it is impossible to speak of certain truths, and those by far the most important of all (being 'metaphysical' in the real sense of the word) in any other language. The language most universally used is that of a geometrical symbolism wherein a dimensionless center is regarded as origin and intersection of three dimensions, each of which can be followed in two opposite directions, so that six directions spring from the origin. They form the three-dimensional cross of which the cruciform symbols used in many traditions are projections. From the point of view of a dweller on this earth—which, since it is inescapably ours, we ignore at our peril—the six directions are not qualitatively equivalent. Two are vertical and four are horizontal; the two vertical directions, upward and downward, are anything but equivalent from any point of view, and of the four horizontal directions, the North-South or polar pair is not equivalent to or interchangeable with the East-West or equatorial pair. Each single direction (North, South, East and West) has its particular qualities derived from the orientation of the earth, and the situation of the individual on the surface of the earth. Because of the analogical relationships existing between different planes of reality, the natural or apparent qualitative differences in the six directions of our terrestrial experience, and their relation to their point of origin and to each other, express adequately—far more adequately than is otherwise possible—the purely qualitative relationships existing on planes other than that to which we are at present confined. Thus, inevitably, the symbolism of the cross permeates not only religion but also our thought and our common speech far more comprehensively than we commonly realize, thereby relating them, consciously or otherwise, both to the purely metaphysical and to the more specifically religious applications of the same symbolism.

That symbolism is not fanciful, but highly realistic. For instance; let us consider an area of the earth's surface small enough to be for practical purposes flat (and few of us are often concerned with larger areas). The rays of the sun descend on to that area. There they initiate and maintain the kind of expansion we call life; but they are interrupted by the surface of the earth and do not penetrate beneath it. Above the surface, all is light and the potentiality of life; at the surface life develops, beneath it, all is darkness and death. Thus the upward direction is that of the source of life, the horizontal is that of the development and expansion of life, and the downward is that of the absence of life. All this is so plainly and evidently factual as scarcely to be worth stating; it is factual independently of what any physicist may have to say about the nature of light or of matter or of their inter-relation, or of the highly relative nature of the conceptions of up and down. The surface of the earth is really the physical plane of reflection of the sun's rays, and on that plane the sun is really the giver of life. For a creature unable to transcend that plane—a plant for instance—there is no other god but the sun.

We as men, alone of all creatures, can transcend the three-dimensional psycho-physical experience, and conceive of something other than the impressions arising out of it. But speech and discursive thought are exclusively derived from and related to our psycho-physical experience, so that when we want to speak of something that transcends it we can only do so by analogy with it; and that is why we have to say that heaven is 'above' and hell 'below', and so on. There is no reason to regret this necessity, for if we were to invent new words having no relation to terrestrial experience whenever we wanted to speak of God or heaven or hell there would be a loss of realism, not only because those words would be less vivid to us, but also because we would deliberately be leaving out of account the very real symbolical relationship existing between the terrestrial plane and other planes. Therefore, the best way of expressing the relationship between the Divine and the terrestrial is to say that the former is 'above' the latter.

There would of course be no point in attempting to justify such usage, based as it is on the natural picture of the universe, merely as means of expression. The need for such justification only arises in connection with the fact that the allegedly unscientific nature of such expressions has been used to support the questioning or rejection of many of the traditional and religious ideas which they have expressed in the past, and still express so adequately today.

Up to this point the formation of a picture of the universe has been regarded as taking place by way of a synthesis of observation, undertaken in order to reveal something of the cause; that is to say as proceeding from the effect towards the cause. It is also possible to approach the matter the other way round, starting from the cause in order to arrive at a view of what the effect really is. If the latter approach, which is the metaphysical approach, is adopted, the resulting picture will be based on something like the considerations that follow, provided that proper allowance is made for the inevitable inadequacy of all forms of expression in this connection.

Nothing is without a cause, so that behind every apparent cause lies another cause, until in the end one arrives at an ultimate cause. There cannot be a plurality of ultimate causes in a single universe, though that universe be limitless in extent and in variety, for if there were more than one, either they would not be ultimate, being related one to another through the universe in question as all secondary causes are, or there would be a plurality of universes each having no relation to or communication with any other. The first alternative brings us back to where we started, and the second has no intelligible significance; therefore the ultimate cause is single. There can be any number of secondary causes, some of which may be, in relation to particular beings or situations, 'relatively ultimate'; but these secondary causes and all things derived from them are permanently present either in act or in potentiality, in the single ultimate cause, which is therefore absolute and indivisible plenitude, without distinction or relativity, subjectivity or objectivity; it is therefore wholly beyond any comparison and is not picturable or nameable. Since by definition the ultimate cause comprehends all possibilities, the possibilities of distinction, separation or imperfection are not excluded from it, despite the fact that they apparently contradict its singleness. Such contradiction cannot however be otherwise than illusory. Existence, etymologically a 'standing apart' from the cause as well as from other things that exist, is the manifestation of those apparently contradictory possibilities. Existence derives all its reality, not from itself, but from the cause that it appears to contradict. In other words, the distinctiveness of all observable and specifiable things arises, not from something that belongs to them, but from the degree and kind of their deprivation. The chain of causality that leads from the cause by way of a succession of deprivations is continuous, so that nothing loses its connection with the cause, if it did so, it would cease to be; but every fresh link in the chain implies a new specification, equivalent to a new kind of obscuration or forgetfulness of the cause, a new veil of illusion between it and man, who, as tradition teaches, was created last and in the image of God. In this sense, then, man himself as a distinctive being, and all that he knows, are but deprivation, forgetfulness and illusion.

Man alone can aspire to dispel the illusion, to see things as they are, to perfect himself. If this aspiration leads him to look at the universe from something like the point of view just outlined, he will realize that the approach to reality is not a movement, the attainment of wisdom is not an achievement, the realization of perfection is not a becoming. All these, which are in essence the same, are but a ceasing to be of that which never was, since its apparent existence was but privation and therefore essentially negative; a ceasing to be of illusion and ignorance.

The Reality is eternal and wholly present everywhere; all that appears to be other than It is forgetfulness of It.

We have but to remember what we are, here and now.

III

The Beauty of Flowers

Flowers which are attractive by reason of their forms, colors or scents have been admired and loved and cultivated for thousands of years; perhaps never more so than in Europe at the present day. Everyone knows, or thinks he knows, what a flower is.

About a hundred years ago the modern scientific point of view began to be applied to flowers. It is necessary to take that point of view into account, because today so many people think that it is the only point of view from which we can learn what a flower really is, or assign to it its proper place in the scheme of things.

From a scientific point of view a flower is characteristic of all the class of Angiosperms. Whether it be conspicuous and attractive or not, it is primarily a mechanism for securing the transfer of pollen from the anther of one flower to the stigma of another of the same species. In the case of conspicuous flowers, this usually takes place on the body of an insect. The form, color and fragrance of flowers is thought to have been evolved in nature for the purpose of attracting insects, the intervention of which compensates for the immobility of plants and makes the impregnation of the ovule by the pollen of a distant individual possible. Alternatively, as everyone knows, pollen may be transported by wind; in such cases the flower is usually small and inconspicuous, though the inflorescence may be beautiful in our eyes. From the scientific point of view, flowers have evolved into what they are solely as a result of the interaction of factors connected with the relationship of plants to insects or to wind.

Insofar as flowers are the indispensable precursors of useful seeds and fruits, with honey as a by-product in some cases, there is an obvious economic relationship between flowers and mankind. Man has taken advantage of the fact that flowers seem to us beautiful, and has tried to accentuate the pleasurable aspects of his relationship to flowers in his development of floriculture. Scientifically speaking, all other kinds of relationship, aesthetic or otherwise, can only be regarded as accidental.

The modern scientific point of view takes account of nothing but the immediate and tangible advantage, 'economic' in the broad sense of the word, to the individual or to the race. It could therefore be described as purely utilitarian. It assumes that the qualities and way of life of every living being, including man, can in principle be regarded primarily as expedients for securing the continuity of the existence of the being or its race or species in the face of environmental pressures and competition from other beings or races. If any other influences are admitted they are regarded as secondary.

There are some scientists and philosophers of science who would say that even the above statement is tendentious, in that it makes use of such words as 'advantage', 'expedients' and 'competition', and thereby suggests some kind of underlying purpose in the process of evolution and in existence generally. To them, there is no such purpose, terrestrial life having arisen purely through a fortuitous combination of circumstances, probably unique, and certainly destined eventually to be swallowed up in some equally fortuitous cataclysm. According to this view there exist only blind forces acting upon elementary particles, the resulting associations and dissociations of which constitute the universe and all that it contains. Thus all our experience, all our aspirations, every conception of beauty or goodness or greatness or of any kind of purpose, and of course any kind of theistic conception, can have no ultimate significance whatever.

This is the philosophy of despair, of which Bertrand Russell is one of the chief exponents. It claims to expound the only intellectually acceptable basis for the development of a philosophy of life, and to represent the only possible logical and intelligent deduction from the discoveries of modern science.[1]

---

1. The main characteristics and conclusions of the evolutionary hypothesis remain much the same, whether the process of evolution be regarded as being with or without some ultimate significance.

Independently of whether they are prepared to accept any particular religious or quasi-religious eschatology, there are probably very few people who can accept in their hearts the view that existence is ultimately meaningless. But the conception of terrestrial life as a struggle for existence, in which every creature or race is fighting for its own advantage, has been thoroughly instilled into our minds by the protagonists of evolutionary ideas.

It is of interest in passing to compare this point of view with another that was very prevalent in the nineteenth century, according to which everything on earth was created, not for its own advantage, nor for the advantage of its race, but for the benefit of mankind. It differed from the evolutionist point of view in being 'creationist', and ostensibly founded on a religious rather than a scientific outlook. It perished partly because creationism was superseded by evolutionism, and partly because it met with insuperable difficulties in application. It was necessary to argue that not only many things apparently useless to man, but also his worst enemies, were in fact created for his special and exclusive benefit. It was however very close to the evolutionist point of view in being essentially utilitarian. Both are examples of the tendency to try to account for everything in terms of immediate and tangible advantage and disadvantage. This is none other than the materialist tendency.

Considerations of immediate advantage and disadvantage can be important in terrestrial life, but any theory founded on them alone is totally insufficient to account for the forms and the behavior of living beings, vegetable, animal and especially human, and no less insufficient to account for their existence, their variety and their qualities, and not least for their beauty. Beauty is the quality that particularly appeals to us in flowers.

The conception of a universal struggle for existence is highly anthropomorphic. It seems probable that our view of the world of nature as a conflict rather than a harmony is little more than evidence of our own state of mind. It is colored far more strongly than we suppose by that state of mind, whether it be internally harmonious or internally distraught. The picture of flowers manifests a joyous superfluity that accords ill with any conception so grim as that of a universal struggle for existence taken as the influence which has made that picture what it is and has conferred on us the inexplicable and gratuitous benediction of flowers.

Struggle there is, obviously; but it is a result of the temporal limitations that obscure the underlying harmony, the harmony that shines forth from within in the inexplicable beauty of flowers. The struggle is as it were superficial; it does not constitute the basic force that moulds the world of nature, still less did it produce the beauty of flowers. The 'struggle for existence' theory is that the more brilliant the flower the better its chances of attracting insects and thereby ensuring pollination and the perpetuation of its race. It sounds plausible, but it does not fit the facts. The attractiveness of flowers to insects bears little relation to their brilliance or size. Lubbock pulled the petals off geraniums and found that insects visited them as before. The flowers of vines, of ivy, of box, of gooseberries, of sycamores, are small and green, yet they are objects of hot competition in the insect world, more so perhaps than most conspicuous flowers. *Cotoneaster horizontalis* has the least conspicuous flowers of any of its race, and is much the most attractive to insects. Neither lilies nor magnolias seem to be particularly attractive, whereas roses and poppies and peonies are. There are also contrasts like that between the fig and the yucca, each dependent for pollination on one species of insect, small and specialized: the flowers of the fig are entirely hidden; the large white flowers of the yucca are flaunted in great plumes on stems many feet high. An abundant source of sugar, like the waste from a sugar factory, unadvertised though it be, is far more attractive to bees than the brightest of flowers. In short, the colors and forms of uncultivated flowers cannot be accounted for solely by any theory that confines its attention to their purely functional or utilitarian aspect.

Let us then assume without more ado that the beauty and fragrance of flowers is not an accident nor yet is it manifested for the exclusive and tangible benefit either of the plants themselves or of man. It can of course be maintained, with no possibility of proof either way, that man alone sees beauty as such; it is anyhow a commonplace that all men do not see it in the same way and that some appear to be totally indifferent to it. Hence the saying that beauty is in the eye of the beholder, and so in one sense it is, but this saying can be interpreted in two different ways. On the one hand, it can mean that beauty is purely subjective and therefore has no intrinsic reality independently of its observer, or, on the other hand, that it has an intrinsic reality but that reality is accessible to an individual only to the extent that he is attuned to it.

According to the first interpretation beauty is less than man and is a product of his nature, according to the second it is greater, or at least more universal, than the human individuality as such. The first interpretation is concordant with the scientific and evolutionary outlook. The second is not, because it takes account of something that is outside the purview of science. It implies that beauty is objective and universal, that its reality is independent of its manifestation in nature, and that therefore it is inherently mysterious, intangible and non-measurable.

If that is so, beauty is by no means a fortuitous attribute of matter; it is something of the universal manifested in the relative. It is a manifestation of the infinite in the finite, and in that case, the real importance of beauty to us does not reside in its pleasurable or aesthetic aspect, but in its symbolism, or in its didactic potentiality.

The traditional association of beauty with truth is then neither sentimental nor fanciful, for the positive qualities, among which is beauty, are immutable realities. Only the material and perishable forms, through which the everpresent potentialities of the qualities may be more or less imperfectly manifested, are ephemeral. Materialism consists precisely in restricting attention to the perishable form. Whether in its scientific or in its popular guise, it is therefore opposed to all that a religion not tainted with materialism teaches, namely, that the material world can only be accounted for in terms of the non-material, the visible in terms of the invisible, the measurable in terms of the non-measurable; and further that the ultimate truth is enshrined in the latter and not in the former.

This is no way implies that material and measurable things should be ignored or despised, but simply that they should be seen for what they are, namely, signs or symbols of a reality immeasurably greater, more comprehensive and more enduring than they are, even in their totality. Here, as always, it is a case of preserving a right balance. This can only be done by keeping the essential principles always in view and interpreting the facts of observation accordingly.

The main principle here in view is the metaphysical superiority or transcendence of the intangible and non-measurable over the tangible and measurable, that is to say, of quality over quantity.

Without quantity the universe as we know it could have no existence. Qualities would remain as unmanifested potentialities. Without quality, if anything could then be said to exist, it would have no intelligibility, it would have the completely abstract character of pure number, to which, as René Guénon has shown, the conception of quantity is in the last analysis reducible. Such a situation is not, strictly speaking, conceivable, since one cannot form a conception of unrelieved indistinction, pure chaos. For similar reasons it is not realizable. Nevertheless it is the situation towards which the world is moving, though it can never attain to it fully.

It is not really surprising that an inversion of priorities has culminated, quite logically, in a sort of nihilism, in the philosophy of 'unyielding despair' which Bertrand Russell announced specifically, and others of the same persuasion by implication, as the only rational basis for the ordering of human life. If the priorities are kept in the right order, the beauty of flowers, seen as the expression of a principle and not as an accident, can teach us directly, intellectually, and without recourse to sentiment of any kind, that this philosophy of despair is rubbish.

Can one thus metaphorically consign to the waste-paper basket the life's work of so many able and erudite men, highly trained in logic and in exposition, and deeply convinced that they are struggling to save mankind from self-destruction? What have they done to deserve such treatment? Well, what they have done is to consign to the waste-paper basket, metaphorically or otherwise, the whole of the 'perennial philosophy' that is enshrined in the sacred Scriptures of the world, all the exposition and exemplification of that philosophy given by the saints and sages whom the world has revered from time immemorial, all religion, all tradition, in short, all that has hitherto given meaning to human life. And, one must add, all that can still give it meaning; not a spurious meaning, as they would have it, but the only true meaning it has.

If they are right, they themselves must be the avatars and the prophets of a new age of realism, destined to replace millennia of delusion; but if they are wrong, the word 'rubbish' applied to their work is too gentle. It is not their erudition that is in question, nor their logical consistency, nor yet their sincerity (for 'sincerity' in its current sense makes no distinction between error and truth); it is the fundamental assumptions on which the logical structure of their philosophy is built.

In the case of the two philosophies here contrasted, their respective starting-points are diametrically opposed, so that, even when there is a superficial resemblance in method or in development, there is still in reality no common measure between them. The one seeks to derive principles from phenomena, the other seeks to see phenomena in the light of their metaphysical principles. The first attempts an impossible task and consequently ends up in a sort of chaos or nihilism; the second attempts a task of supreme difficulty and one that can never be fully accomplished, least of all by the unaided efforts of man, but it is the task that justifies all other tasks.

Scientifically speaking, all other kinds of relationship, aesthetic or otherwise, can only be regarded as accidental.

Somebody may say: 'Are you not doing exactly what you criticize, and trying to arrive at a principle by studying a phenomenon, for surely beauty is a phenomenon, since it is observable.'

Any such question misses the point that beauty as such is not a phenomenon and is not observable, what is observable is the material or psychic entity through which beauty is manifested in some degree and in some mode. The endless variety of its modes, in each of which it can achieve a sort of perfection that reflects its universality, bears witness to that very universality, to the fact that beauty is in its essence a principle and not an accident, whether it be manifested in a flower or in a star or in a human soul.

To say that beauty is a principle or an archetypal possibility of the highest metaphysical importance, adds nothing to the direct and incalculable impact of our experience of it. That experience can to a greater or less extent carry us 'out of ourselves' by giving us a glimpse of something greater than ourselves, though its vehicle may be only a humble flower. To the extent that it does so, it is an experience of the 'supernatural', whether we recognize it as such or not. Beauty is necessarily something like that, or else it is but a perishable illusion devoid of ultimate significance. If it is devoid of ultimate significance, then so is everything else, ourselves included. A rejection of the supernatural logically and inevitably leads to something like a philosophy of despair.[2] The certitudes or basic assumptions that provide the starting-points of logic are necessarily themselves supra-logical, in the sense that, like existence itself or the beauty of a flower, they cannot themselves be objects of discursive proof.

There are a few people to whom flowers make no appeal. People's likes and dislikes in relation to flowers are different. The same is of course true of the perception of beauty in its many other forms. These commonplace facts may seem to support the idea that the whole issue turns on the vagaries of individual taste. But if beauty is what it has been said to be in the preceding paragraphs, its universality and transcendence imply that there must be some real or quasi-absolute criterion whereby it can in principle be judged. The distinction between good and bad taste cannot be wholly arbitrary, nor a matter of fashion or period alone, nor even of the application of any purely human standards of judgment. Distinctions of taste which arise entirely from individual or collective peculiarities are indeed of a very limited and fugitive importance. Other distinctions can however reveal differences of approach that are more profound, because they are connected with the didactic or symbolical aspects of their objects. Distinctions of taste in the floral domain are by no means always of the first kind alone; they may indeed be more revealing than distinctions applied to human artifacts, because they are uncomplicated by local or national differences of style and technique.

---

2. One could wish that those whose religion implies an acceptance of the supernatural would apply the same kind of logic to the development of their certitude as its rejecters apply to theirs, instead of always trying to justify it in terms of morality or of contingent advantage, which, in the nature of the case, it is impossible to do conclusively.

In certain circumstances the symbolical aspect of a particular flower predominates, but that occurs only when it is used as part of some formal and established religious or traditional symbolism. One could instance the rose in the center of the cross, where the five-petalled flower symbolizes the 'quintessence,' the unmanifested *quinta essentia* which is central to the four elements and is their principle; the lotus as the throne of the Buddha, horizontal but with upturned petals, and lying on the face of the waters; or the *fleur-de-lys*, which we now know as iris, and the association of its triple form with the Trinity. In such cases the symbolism associated with each flower could be called a specialized symbolism, to which the beauty of the flower is incidental.

Here however, we are chiefly concerned with the general symbolism of flowers in its less specialized manifestations, and with the relationship of that symbolism to what would usually be regarded purely as questions of individual or collective taste.

One aspect of the general symbolism of flowers which is often overlooked is the following. As everybody knows, the function of flowers is exclusively concerned with the sexual reproduction of plants. In general those parts of a flower which we most admire, such as the petals, are secondary sexual characters, closely associated with the minute primary characters. The whole assembly is paraded and flaunted with joyful unconcern above the more mundane structural and nutritive organs, and it constitutes what is usually for us the most attractive feature of the plant. In this way flowers exemplify more completely and perfectly than any other living organisms the primordial innocence, beauty and unselfconsciousness of the sexual function. As a symbol and as something like a perpetual renewal of the primordial Act of creation, that function is essentially sacred; but it can be profaned and prostituted by fallen man, who has lost his innocence and unselfconsciousness and can by no means recover them. The traditional restrictions and taboos which surround the sexual function in all human societies take account of these facts. To many people, especially in these days, those restrictions seem harsh and futile, or even psychologically unsound, but they are adapted to the present needs of fallen man, and above all to the safeguarding of the fate of his soul. The latter consideration plays almost no part in contemporary discussions of what has become a burning question, but it is by far the most important, outweighing all considerations of present ease.

A conscious conformity to God's laws is required of us, in exchange for our gift of free will. The beauty of a perfect but unconscious conformity is demonstrated in flowers, here and now, as a perishable symbol of that which awaits in eternity those whose conformity in this life is fully conscious.

Each manifestation of floral beauty is in some degree unique and incomparable. A wild rose, a Madonna lily, the Pasque flower, the common primrose, most crocus species, fritillaries, lily-of-the-valley, a wild cherry or apple (the latter in its true wild form is rare), Grass of Parnassus... But why continue? for the list might never end; but it can at least be restricted by considering only flowers that grow wild or can be cultivated out of doors in Britain.

Each of the flowers named is like nothing else, and it is no use attempting to compare one with another. The writer is well aware that his own individual preferences have played a large part in the choice of those mentioned, but those preferences do not signify. Some readers may wish to delete, and some to add, but that also does not signify, provided that any plant named manifests a beauty all its own, beyond compare, or, as we so significantly say, 'out of this world.'

There are also many less conspicuous flowers that would qualify for inclusion if they were looked at carefully enough, not least the grasses and sedges, in which beauty of form is emphasized by a relative uniformity of color. And again there are many others which are indispensable as foils or backgrounds to set off the beauty of their brighter fellows, such as the Umbelliferae, the clovers, the bedstraws and so on. The picture is one of an endless variety of degrees and kinds of perfection, some really incomparable—that is to say, limited only by the fact that they exclude other perfections—and others of lower degree and limited in other ways. It is not wrong to use the word 'perfection' in this way, although, according to the strict meaning of the word, it is an absolute and as such cannot be limited. But we are speaking of the world, and that is exactly what the world is; perfection manifested in imperfection, the absolute in the relative, the infinite in the finite; every part of the world mirrors the whole. The paradoxical or mysterious or miraculous character of the world is reflected in the gaiety, the subtlety and the extravagance of its flowers at least as clearly as in any other way.

A gardener or botanist may have noticed that all the flowers so far mentioned are species, that is to say that they occur as wild plants in this or in some other country. They are not among the innumerable hybrids or varieties that occur only in cultivation and are now conveniently described as 'cultivars'. These cultivars are the result of a conscious endeavor to enhance the pleasure given by flowers by selecting forms that are larger or brighter in color or more striking in form than the wild species from which they are derived; also by providing the gardener or the buyer of flowers with a much wider choice than he could obtain if he had to rely on species alone.

These cultivars are commonly referred to as 'improved' varieties; perhaps the commonest and the oldest kind of 'improvement' consists in a multiplication of the petals, resulting in what we call a 'double' flower. Double flowers, and flowers showing unusual size or brilliance as well as other departures from the normal occur occasionally in nature, and the development of most cultivars has started by the selection of such 'sports'. Their peculiarities can often be accentuated under the conditions of intensive cultivation. It is this possibility of artificial selection, often resulting in great changes in the outward forms of plants, which provided Darwin with the basis of his theory of natural selection.

Whatever may be the explanation of the beauty of wild flowers, there can be no doubt that there is a conscious purpose behind the changes brought about by cultivation; it is of course the satisfaction of the desires of mankind. As those desires have never before been so ambitious as they are today, nor the means of satisfying them so easy to come by, so it is with flowers. The contemporary desire for novelty, for sensationalism, for quantity (which includes size as well as number) is catered for by new methods of inducing variations and of speedy propagation.

To what extent and in what sense can the results of the work of flower breeders past and present properly be designated 'improvement'? That work has produced many long-established favorites, the double roses and pinks, the enlarged lily-of-the-valley, the endless variety of pansies, primroses, and auriculas, the double peonies, the chrysanthemums and dahlias, fuchsias and geraniums, tulips, irises, and so on. Some of these are seen in almost every garden, and no wonder, because they have endless brilliance and charm. They are however in danger of being superseded by more recent introductions, the bewildering multiplicity of which is presented to us in innumerable catalogues in which the resources of language are strained to the utmost to describe their striking colors, gigantic size and sensational effect.

Without attempting to deny that some of these sensational novelties are beautiful, occasionally very beautiful, it may yet be permissible to suggest that in too many cases more has been lost than has been gained. The new floribunda roses do not belie their name, but most of them are shapeless and often unbelievably crude in color; the total effect of a bed of modern roses is indeed startling, but it may be little else. The latest gladioli have the same faults, the new daffodils look like artificial flowers which in a sense they are; cyclamens, among the most subtly elegant of flowers, have become enormous, distorted and even frilled, pansies have become huge and floppy, polyanthus primrose gigantic, sometimes frilled and even pink in color, losing all their characteristic decisive neatness, the regal pelargoniums had comparable qualities but are suffering exactly the same fate. One has sometimes got to look at the leaves to see whether a flower is a pelargonium or a petunia or a hibiscus or what. Delphiniums, larkspurs, clarkias, godetias have become like solid columns of colored crinkly paper, losing all their pristine elegance of form and marking. In short the general tendency is all towards the substitution of ostentation for elegance, crudity for subtlety, blatancy for beauty, quantity for quality. People do not seem to want to look at a flower, they want to be hit in the eye by it. The frequent sacrifice of scent to gaudiness is often lamented, but it seems equally often to be accepted as inevitable.

The concerns just expressed about what is happening to garden flowers are fairly widespread although those who hold them are in a minority. The 'improved' varieties are on the whole much the most popular, and that is what makes it worthwhile for the nurseryman to produce them. The word 'vulgar' simply means 'popular', and popular is precisely what the taste of the majority inevitably is and always will be. We saw earlier that, beauty being what it is, the criteria of taste can never be wholly arbitrary, despite the fact that individual and collective peculiarities and fashions play a very large part in establishing them in any particular case. Those criteria cannot be defined only in terms of human reactions; the ultimate criteria can only be sought in the field of symbolism, for it is through their symbolism alone that the phenomena of this world bring us into contact with the absolute.

Now it can be asserted that the symbolism of the natural is always more direct than that of the artificial, although this does not necessarily imply that whatever is man-made in whole or in part must always in all circumstances be rejected in favor of the natural, for man was not given his faculties and powers for nothing.

The natural is nevertheless always nearer to its origin, and its origin is the Origin of all things. The work of man, or man's interference with the natural, when it is directed mainly to the satisfaction of his own desires and fancies, always tends towards forgetfulness of the Origin. This forgetfulness grows as man takes more and more pride in his own supposed originality or 'creativity'. In fact no man ever created anything. The most any man can do is to play about with material and rearrange it for his advantage or amusement. However, for so long as man does not lose sight of the Origin of his material, nor of the fact that its Origin is also his own—and this implies among other things that he does not lose his humility—his work may be legitimate.[3]

Up to a point, then, the deliberate rearrangement, encouragement or suppression of potentialities present in living things—

---

3. The author wrote in a letter to a friend about his garden: '*The important thing is to understand why it is worthwhile to make a garden—why a garden is (or can be) much more than just a pleasure for the senses. The reason is this. God allows us to do our best to imitate His Paradise, however incompletely, provided that we never forget that all beauty comes from Him alone and remains always in Him, without any loss and for ever.*'

flowering plants for example—all lead to a certain enrichment at not too heavy a cost; although the enrichment tends to be quantitative and the loss to be qualitative. Inevitably there comes a point at which the balance tips, and thereafter erroneous tendencies reinforce one another, so that not only do losses outweigh gains, but even those gains themselves prove unsatisfying, and must constantly be replaced by others. All this is aggravated by the intrusion of commercialism, with its large-scale mechanized operations, standardization and advertising. In the end commercialism may become virtually the dictator of taste.

That being so, one can see why the improved varieties produced in the earlier years of plant breeding are likely to be qualitatively superior to later productions. The old-fashioned roses, the cottage pinks and carnations, the double stocks, and many other old favorites, although very artificial in that they are very 'double', are nevertheless still a little 'out of this world', and so are the auriculas, pansies and violas; their beauty is subtle and mysterious even when they are very 'showy'. The same could be said of many of the Japanese ornamental cherries, maples and peonies. Nevertheless, the enrichment represented by these more or less ancient cultivars, as well as by many of the less vulgar of their successors, is nearly always in the realm of the quantitative and sensual; the corresponding impoverishment is always in the realm of the qualitative and symbolical. And so one can see how once again the prevailing tendencies of the day are reflected in the floral domain, this time in the department of floriculture. If they are reflected less intensely there than they are in some other sectors of the field of visual aesthetics—notably in painting and sculpture—it is because the material used is the living plant, which must at least remain alive, and while it does so can never lose all its natural characteristics.

Added to the ever-growing array of new cultivars available to gardeners, is a vast number of alien species, introduced into this country from all over the world in the past hundred years or so. A few of them have established themselves firmly in our gardens, as firmly as older introductions such as tulips, lilacs, peonies and roses, and no less worthily. We should be poorer without *Viburnum fragrans*, the regal lily, the blue-poppy, and some of the new Rhododendrons, to mention only a few of those most widely cultivated. In all, hundreds, even thousands, of exotic species are cultivated by enthusiasts and admired by many more. The hybridizers are of course hard at work 'improving' them, especially the lilies.

It has been said that a greater variety of plants can be grown in the British Isles than in any comparable area in the world, and this is probably not far wrong. Here indeed is a tremendous enrichment, horticulturally speaking; it may represent something like an *embarras de richesses*: but if so, it is surely of a fairly harmless kind. But it is confined to the relatively restricted and artificial domain of horticulture, and it is a poor compensation for another result of the artificiality of modern life, the depletion of our wild flowers.

The demand for land for residential, industrial and recreational uses, chemical methods of weed control on farms and elsewhere and the invasion of the countryside by a motorized proletariat, pathetically longing for virgin nature but threatening its continued existence, these and other factors are resulting in an appallingly rapid depletion of wild flowers both in quantity and in variety. The creation of 'nature reserves', desirable though it be, like many other attempts to preserve a precious heritage, cannot restore that heritage. It can only preserve it as a museum specimen, no longer alive, though better than nothing.

Not only the longing for virgin nature, but also the cult of flowers so prevalent today, are above all signs of an unconscious reaction against the ugliness associated with so many of the products of an industrialized society; and that ugliness is itself a sign, a sign of the hatefulness of all that brings it about.

If a modern town were in conformity with the real needs and destiny of its inhabitants, they would love it and seek it, instead of getting out of it into the country or to the seaside at every available opportunity, often at the cost of discomfort and inconvenience. But when they do they cannot help bringing the town out with them; the car, the radio, the newspapers, the cartons; and in doing so they gradually destroy the very thing they are seeking. That thing is in the last analysis, did they but know it, not so much natural beauty as communion with God. It is this, too, that the lover of flowers is really seeking, and if he knew it, he would not be so keen as he is on their supposed 'improvement'; he would be more ready to accept and to marvel, and perhaps to understand.

It is mainly field botanists and Nature Conservation societies who are aware of and lament the elimination, except in a few carefully guarded sites, of many of our rarer plants, such as the Pasque flower, the fritillary and numerous orchids. Obvious to all is the reduction in buttercups, ox-eye daisies, harebell, primrose, cowslip, meadow saxifrage, wild daffodil, in short, of almost everything that formerly made our meadows flowery. There is also the more equivocal case of the weeds of arable land. Charlock may be dismissed as both vicious and ugly, but the poppy, the corn-cockle, the corn marigold, the bindweed and the cornflower have been deservedly admired, though harmful to the crops with which they compete. Under the older farming methods they could usually be kept more or less in check but they could not be eliminated; modern methods are more comprehensive. These weeds, together with their no less numerous and troublesome but less visually attractive companions in the field, are not defeated yet; but if modern chemical methods are pursued and developed for a few more decades they may well be virtually eliminated.

The most recent development consists in the invention of plastic flowers. By the use of modern techniques the most conspicuous features of the forms and colors of natural or cultivated flowers can be imitated very closely; this applies particularly to lilies. If the broad decorative effect of floral arrangements were the sole criterion of the value of flowers, it would be difficult to find any plausible objection to the use of plastic flowers in appropriate circumstances. They last for ever, they need no messy water to keep them going, they are washable and can be packed away when not in use, and they eliminate all the recurrent trouble and expense associated with real flowers.

The artificial flowers of the past were usually recognizable as such and did not pretend to be anything else; they were indeed often products of a real art; one could instance the charming 'flowers' made out of shells in the Far East, which are the products of a gentle and unassuming form of decorative art that charms without deceiving. It is precisely their deceptiveness that condemns plastic flowers.

They represent an attempt at a complete and conclusive replacement of the works of God by the works of man, a more and more complete obscuring of the reality by the appearance, a further substitution of the spurious but plausible for the genuine and guileless, death masquerading more and more successfully as life. They are like a frozen smile on the face of a corpse. Their use in churches in substitution for real flowers is nothing less than a desecration; their use elsewhere is a manifestation of bad taste pure and simple, and is correspondingly significant.

In conspicuous contrast to the durability of plastic flowers is the evanescence of real flowers. Among the innumerable types of beauty in this world, that of flowers is both the most widespread and the most untarnished, and at the same time it is one of the least durable. The ephemerality of natural flowers is only that of the material forms through which their beauty is manifested, and does not appertain to beauty as such. Those forms are continually and rhythmically renewed. This year's dog-rose is not the same as last year's, but its beauty is the same; the quality is eternal, only its manifestation in a material form is ephemeral.

The theme of the perishability of all forms and of their rhythmical renewal is frequent in the sacred scriptures of the world. Existence is joined to eternity not only through the qualities manifested in it, but also through its rhythms, which, as it were, compensate the irreversible and devouring character of time. We can sense this directly when the repeated and identical vibrations of a string produce a single musical note. Through flowers as through music we can perhaps learn to hear something of the 'music of the spheres', wherein the rhythms of the whole creation are unified in one great song of praise.

Reginald Farrer, a great gardener and plant collector who introduced many plants from the Far East, wrote from a high alpine meadow in China in 1918:

> And if, amid the cataclysms of anguish that clamor round us everywhere nowadays, you declare that all this babble about beauty and flowers is a vain impertinence, then I must tell you that you err, and that your perspectives are false. Mortal dooms

and dynasties are brief things, but beauty is indestructible and eternal, if its tabernacle be only a petal that is shed tomorrow. Wars and agonies are shadows only cast across the path of man: each successive one seems the end of all things, but man perpetually emerges and goes forward, lured always and cheered and inspired by the immortal beauty-thought that finds form in all the hopes and enjoyments of his life. *Inter arma silent flores* is no truth; on the contrary, amid the crash of doom our sanity and survival more than ever depend on the strength with which we can listen to the still small voice that towers above the cannons, and cling to the little quiet things of life, the things that come and go and yet are always there, the inextinguishable lamps of God amid the disaster that man has made of his life.[4]

The evanescence of flowers is not a matter for regret. It is an ever-present reminder of what we are. Their recurrence is at the same time a guarantee of the immutability of the qualities that so delight us in them.

The reality that can be discerned through the symbolism of flowers is itself something that can only be apprehended directly, just as their beauty is apprehended; it cannot be attained by the analytical or imaginative powers of the mind alone, and it cannot be contained by any formula. An understanding of symbolism and reflection thereon is very far from being useless, but it cannot by itself either take the place of, or bring about, the direct apprehension of reality that is prefigured in our natural and unaffected delight in flowers.

One day the disciples of the Buddha were assembled to hear him preach a sermon. But he said not a word. Instead, he stooped down and plucked a flower and held it up for them to see. Of all that assembly, only one showed by his smile that he understood.

---

4. *The Rainbow Bridge* (London: E. Arnold & Co., 1919, p 225).

IV
Being Oneself

If the observations in this chapter are addressed to the reader in person, it is because the question dealt with concerns only the individual as such, as it were in his relationship to himself. It is not abstract, theoretical and remote, but immediate and personal. It arises out of the advice, so lavishly bestowed on us all in these days, to the effect that, since pretence and hypocrisy are odious, it is above all necessary to 'be oneself'. This advice seems simple enough until one begins to wonder exactly how to apply it to one's own case. For you, the reader, 'one's own case' is your own case, and nobody else's.

What in fact are you, essentially and not accidentally? What are you 'in yourself', and not as butcher, baker, or candlestick-maker? You cannot profitably try to be yourself unless you are sure that you know the answer to that question.

Are you a being created by God in His own image, appointed by him as his representative on earth and accordingly given dominion over it, and equipped for the fulfillment of that function with a relative freedom of choice in both thought and action? Do you have Freedom, which reflects the total absence of constraint attributable to God alone, but at the same time makes you liable to err? Are you essentially that, and only accidentally anything else?

Or, alternatively, are you essentially a specimen of the most advanced product so far known of a continuous and progressive evolution, starting from the fortuitous stringing together of a protein molecule in some warm primeval mud, that mud itself being a rare and more or less fortuitous product of the evolution of the galaxies from a starting point about which the physicists have not yet quite made up their minds?

If you choose the first, the mystical or religious alternative, you do not necessarily exclude *a priori* any plausible description of your physical situation in the Universe. You do however exclude absolutely both the primacy and the finality of any such description. It can never be more than a description, and as such not an explanation, even if it is as complete and as correct as man can make it. So, if you accept the mystical alternative, you must refuse to accept any mere description as an adequate explanation of what you are.

If you choose the second, the physical alternative (and the word 'physical' is here more or less equated to the word 'natural', so that it includes the mind as well as the body) you thereby exclude the first. You then regard your body, your thoughts and your feelings as comprising all that you are, so that whatever may be called 'mystical' or 'religious' can only be explained as a product of these three. If you choose this physical alternative, to 'be yourself' means simply to give free rein to your bodily desires, your thoughts and your feelings. That, in effect, seems to be what you and I, and especially our children, are being advised to do. The consequent disorder often excites our surprise and disapproval. Incidentally, if you do give free rein to these three things, you are playing straight into the hands of anyone who knows how to manipulate them for his own ends. With the aid of modern psychology, that manipulation has become a science.

And yet how right the advice offered to us is! If we are indeed 'made in the image of God', all we need to do is to 'be ourselves'.

If with that end in view you try to find out what you are by looking at yourself, what you appear to yourself to be will be what you are accidentally and not what you are essentially. When you look at yourself, or think that you are doing so, there is one who looks and there is something he sees. They cannot be the same. If they were the same they would be one and not two, so that no relationship, either of 'looking at' or of any other kind could arise. That is why, when you look at yourself, the essential 'you' is really looking only at the accidental 'you'. In other words, you are looking at what would nowadays be called your 'personality'.[1]

Yet you are one person and not two. You are that same one person whatever may happen to you; you remain yourself under all the

---

1. And if you happened to be thinking about 'developing your personality', in the hope that, if you succeeded, you would then 'be yourself' more truly than you are now, you would only be doing the fashionable thing.

vicissitudes that may effect your body or your mind, at least as long as you are sane. Your mind and your body together constitute what is sometimes called your 'psycho-physical complex'. That complex is never the same for two minutes together, either materially or psychically; but your identity remains constant whether you are young or old, fat or thin, happy or miserable, awake or asleep. If that were not so, there would be no continuity in your existence, no individuality and no awareness of change. There is a 'you' that is the invariable point of reference, or center, and there are the changeable things of which it is conscious. The former is not identifiable with the latter. Those changeable things include everything you can perceive and know distinctively, and they are environmental, peripheral or external with respect to the conscious center that is the real 'you'. Your whole psycho-physical complex, insofar as you can perceive and know it distinctively, is evidently among these external and changeable things. It belongs to you, but it is not the 'you' to which it belongs. It is the 'personality' which you may seek to develop, but it is not the 'you' that seeks to develop it.

Therefore, if you want to know what you really are, in order that you may know what it means to 'be yourself', you must direct your attention inwards and not outwards; that is to say, away from all objects of the senses, including your own body, mind and feelings, towards the non-distinguishable central point of your being. This inwardly directed attention must evidently be aimed in a direction opposite to that of outward attention. Outward attention is, precisely, what we call observation. We are all taught nowadays that the only way to ascertain the truth is by way of the intensification and refinement of observation. For most of us therefore inward attention involves something we may never have consciously attempted, or perhaps even considered.

It is true that we cannot live without observation, our senses having no other function. Nevertheless, if what has been said is true, any approach to truth that relies on observation and on nothing else excludes the realization of the most important truth of all, the truth on which all other truths hang, namely, the truth about what we ourselves really are. If we are misled concerning what we are, and therefore concerning what anything else is, and what the purpose of our life is, and what our destiny is, it is not much use knowing anything else, because the chances are that we shall then misapply our knowledge, probably to our own hurt. Is not that obvious? And does it not suggest rather alarmingly exactly what seems to be happening?

You will no doubt already have realized that this other approach to truth, this inward attention or 'concentration' which is as it were the opposite, or the complement to the approach of observation, can be nothing other than the way of contemplation, the way followed by wise and holy men of all ages and peoples. Since its goal cannot be perceived distinctively, this way cannot be mapped out. Those who have followed it, and they alone, can teach it.

If you are not one of those to whom the scientific approach alone is valid, all this will not seem to you mere empty sophistry. It may therefore be worthwhile to try to carry the matter a little farther.

You have probably noticed that to say 'your' essential being may suggest that it belongs to you; that it is even to some extent at your disposal or subject to your influence, as if it were your property. Of course it is not so. Nothing that you can do affects in any way the fact that you are what you are. As we have seen, your essential being remains what it is while the current of changeable and perishable forms flows past it. There is therefore no particular reason to suppose that it is perishable, and moreover, for a believer, there is every reason to suppose that it is not. But your essential being must not be confused with the accidental accretions that are so closely associated with it during its sojourn on earth, including of course your observable psycho-physical complex itself. That is where so many believers get into a muddle when they are considering the posthumous states of the essential being, which are sometimes called 'heaven', 'purgatory', and 'hell'.

One more point. If your 'accidentality' alone is distinguishable while your essentiality is not, the same applies to your neighbor. That suggests that you and he are essentially one and only accidentally two. If you saw the situation in that way you would naturally love him 'as yourself'; but you can only see the situation in that way insofar as you have realized what you yourself are. This realization involves bypassing the ever-changing multiplicity of your terrestrial accidentality and seeking with all your heart and mind and strength the changeless Unity that is the central and essential reality of yourself, of your neighbor and of all beings. And you can only hope to find it where it is to be found, and that is 'within you'.

You do see, don't you, that the words 'being oneself' can be interpreted in two critically different ways?

V

Predestination & Free Will

Modern science, here called 'science' for short, is at once the product, the formal expression and the principal support of the progressive outlook with which it coincides in origin and in development. This outlook now penetrates all departments of life, political, cultural, popular and even religious, as well as the specifically scientific. Insofar as we all share it to some extent, we are all scientists today, even when we are ignorant of the technicalities of science or critical of its results or sensitive to its dangers. The real significance of the development of academic science is to be found, not in its technicalities nor in its practical applications, but in our civilization as a whole, in ourselves. Therefore we cannot understand it without understanding ourselves.

Our human situation in this world incorporates a paradox: the paradox between predestination and free will. Science, and the philosophies derived from it, have so far left this paradox either unconsidered or unresolved. Yet surely it is vastly more important to know what, if anything, is predestined and what is not, and what, if any, are the limits of human free will, than it is to know a lot about the constitution of the physical universe?

The ultimate aim of science is to discover the laws governing the universe, the so-called 'laws of Nature', and to define them in unequivocal terms. Probably no scientist of repute would claim that the attainment of this objective as a whole is even in sight. Yet most scientists would maintain that science is beyond question aiming in the right direction, and that a good start on the right lines has been made. Such, at any rate, is the assumption underlying, not only all our planning, but also almost all our philosophy, both academic and popular.

The 'laws of Nature', as formulated in scientific terms, are in fact no more than descriptions of the inter-relations of observable features of the universe. They are always liable to alteration if, as often happens, more accurate or more refined observations reveal a flaw in a description. However, the use of the word 'law' in this sense is well established, and it would be inconvenient to discard it altogether. The earliest of such laws to be formulated scientifically were those of mechanics, closely followed by the laws of physics (excluding the very recent atomic physics). In these fields precise mathematical formulation is possible, and consequently the behavior of the objects studied can be predicted with certainty,[1] provided only that all the conditions obtaining in any particular case can be precisely specified. The unambiguous precision of the laws of mechanics has made them the model, first of the laws of physics, then of all scientific laws. It has been the aim of science to follow that model in all its branches, not excepting, for instance, in its biological, psychological and sociological ramifications, hoping thus to achieve in the end a comparable mathematical exactitude in all of them, while at the same time establishing a basis for their inter-relation. That basis would inevitably be quantitative, since only the quantitative aspect

---

1. This statement might appear to be contradicted by Heisenberg's so-called 'uncertainty principle', and other more recent hypotheses postulating an element of uncertainty or unpredictability or causelessness in certain changes taking place on a sub-atomic scale. The laws of Nature then become the result of probabilities, so high as to amount to certainty, the certainty that the effects of the changes in question will average out. If indeed real events can take place for no reason at all, the philosophical implications of the fact cannot be negligible. One wonders however if they are real events, rather than images suggested by the employment of mathematical expedients, akin perhaps to the 'randomization' of data that are to be subjected to statistical analysis. However that may be, their most evident philosophical implication is anything but new, namely, that in the domain of relativity, which coincides with the domain of science, we are necessarily concerned only with probabilities and not with certainty. Certainty resides only in the absolute, and the science concerned with that domain is the science of metaphysics, on which modern science can have nothing to say. This fact is obscured, but not invalidated, by a widespread incomprehension, both popular and academic, of the true nature of metaphysics.

of things can be expressed in unequivocal terms, the type of such expressions being the mathematical formula. The ultimate aim is in fact to describe the universe by reducing it to a formula, or system of formulae, as nearly as possible mathematical in their precision.

If the universe can in principle be described in some such way, it is only necessary to discover the relevant formulae in order to be able to predict the future with certainty. The approach and methods of science are consistent with the assumption that the universe is in fact constituted in that way. They are inconsistent with any other assumption. If that assumption were correct, the course of all events both great and small would be rigidly conditioned by unchanging laws, and if that were so, no alternative possibilities could ever present themselves in any domain. In that case, what appears to us as chance or uncertainty does so only because we do not yet know all the laws. The freedom of the human will to change the course of events must then be a delusion, though it seems to us to be one of the most obvious facts of our experience.

We do not at all like the idea of being 'really' something like machines, obedient to ineluctable laws, and not 'really' eating or saying what we choose to eat or say, nor 'really' turning this way and that at our pleasure. But if science is working on the right lines, even our apparent free will must some day be fitted into the system, and thus be revealed as a strict conformity to law. Either that, or mankind is not after all subject to the same laws as the rest of the universe.[2] In short: the universe, and man with it, is either governed by laws that are in principle ascertainable and definable or it is not. Science cannot have it both ways, and in trying to do so it throws into high relief the classical antinomy between predestination and free will.

Science uses its free will, its power of choice, to build up a system in which free will can have no place. It does not seem to be noticed that if the world does indeed constitute a quasi-mechanical system, such that it could, in theory even if not in practice, be the subject of

---

2. In that case however science must admit that there is a domain, and from a human point of view a critically important one, to which its approach and its methods are not applicable.

a complete specification, it must be that sort of system already, independently of what we know or do not know about it. In that case all change is predestined and changes now taking place do so as it were mechanically, whether we understand the reasons for them or not. What is more, if we did understand those reasons we could no nothing that could affect in any way our own situation or any other. If that were true, our present attitude, which is one of supposing that we can, would be really rather pathetic.

An apologist for the scientific point of view might retort more or less as follows: we must take things as we find them, and ourselves as we find ourselves; it would be unscientific to do otherwise. It is a fact of observation that we appear to have some degree of free will, so that we can at least to some extent influence the course of events. Our endeavors as scientists are in fact largely directed towards increasing our power of doing so. Although at present we have to work with the fact that the chain of events, particularly in certain fields, is not predictable in practice, we do want to make it as nearly predictable as we can. As to precisely what is predestined and what is not, we cannot say until we know a good deal more than we do now. Let philosophers worry themselves about such matters, while we get on with our job.

The answer to that sort of argument is that the scientist is not taking things as he finds them if he confines his efforts to the building up of a system in which free will can have no place, or at most a provisional and temporary place. He is doing one of two things: either he is assuming that human free will will some day be brought into the system, despite the fact that its existence appears to contradict the very principles on which that system is built; or he is simply ignoring the question because free will cannot be made to fit into his system. In either case he can scarcely claim that he is being scientific, that is to say, that he is taking up the position of a detached and unprejudiced observer. The claim to being detached fails on the grounds that it is impossible that he should detach himself from the central position he occupies in relation to any picture of reality he may arrive at, since without him there would be no picture. The claim to be unprejudiced fails on the grounds that he is deliberately by-passing a fact of observation and choosing to adopt the scientific approach to reality because it has produced remarkable results in certain directions, even though it is not the only approach possible and its long-term results have yet to be ascertained.

In spite of many advantages on the material plane, the advance of science does not seem to have made us any happier or more secure than we were. Most people think that this is because science has not yet advanced far enough. May it not in fact be because the approach of science is blind to certain essential factors, and incapable of seeing what these factors really are?

Science must be right in supposing that, if there were no fundamental and all-embracing laws or principles, the universe would be chaotic and not, as it is, a cosmos continuous in time and coherent in space. So how can science be mistaken? It can only be so mistaken in its insistence that the ultimate cause and meaning, and all the laws of the universe can be definable in scientific terms. Science seeks to discover and to define the laws of Nature, and it assumes both that this must be possible and also that nothing can properly be called a law or a principle unless it can be defined.

To define anything is to state as precisely as possible what are its limits, so that its extent and its nature may be specified. There is in fact only one thing that can be specified absolutely and unequivocally, and independently of any human viewpoint, and that is pure number. This is because number alone is entirely abstract and independent of particularized viewpoints, it alone represents pure quantity and presupposes no qualitative distinction. Therefore only the quantitative aspect of an object is that which is absolutely measurable. All other kinds of measurement or description introduce some qualitative factor or comparison which is not, in the last analysis, reducible to quantity. For instance, the distinction between extension and mass (corresponding to our experience of distance and weight) is qualitative, and it is a vital distinction, since ten miles are not equivalent to ten tons. Scientists would like to be able to express extension and mass in purely mathematical or quantitative terms, so that the physical universe could be as it were reduced to a common denominator.[3]

---

3. But it is safe to say that they never will, because the distinction in question will never be expressible in terms of pure number without reference to any other factor.

Science is always trying to maintain its reputation for exactitude by seeking to express everything as nearly as possible in purely quantitative terms, despite the fact that every distinction—except that between two numbers—has necessarily a qualitative aspect which cannot be expressed in purely quantitative terms without destroying or obscuring its essential nature.

Distinctions between colors, for instance, can be specified in terms of wavelengths, but wavelengths are not colors. It will be said that the experience of color is purely subjective, entirely lacking in a blind or color-blind man, and that it is therefore more or less illusory or unreal, or at least unimportant, and that its ultimate reality resides in whatever of its characteristics can be specified without reference to subjective experiences. The reality of color in fact resides wholly elsewhere, namely in the person who sees.

Where, then, does the reality of other things, for example of extension or of mass, really reside? Is it in our experience of them as distance or weight, or is it in their abstract mathematical formulations? The same question could be asked of space, time and all the other general conditions of our experience. Science says that the abstract formulations alone are purely objective, and that it is they that represent the reality. But science is then equating the objective with the quantitative, as if qualitative distinctions were not objective, and as if it did not itself habitually treat them as such; and at the same time it is equating the subjective with the illusory, as if subject and object were opposites and not complementaries, or as if the word 'object' had any meaning in the absence of a subject, and at the same time as if science itself were not as it were a 'subject' which objectivizes its own impressions in a manner consistent with its own nature and not otherwise.

The findings of science are conceptions; as such they exist nowhere but in the human brain; they therefore correspond to an internal reality as well as to an external reality. If external correspondence alone is treated as significant, the result lacks an essential dimension; though it may be correct as far as it goes. It is as it were exclusively 'horizontal'; like a diagram on paper, it takes no account of the 'vertical' dimension without which nothing is alive and real. When it is supposed that the approach of science alone is able to provide a representation of things as they really are, realism is lost. Then and only then does science become deceptive. Ought not science forthwith to begin asking itself whether it is not itself so to speak 'color-blind', deliberately shutting its eyes to the qualities that make things what they are? [4]

The effect of the predominance of the scientific point of view is thus to detach humanity more and more from all those purely qualitative—and therefore inherently non-measurable—characteristics and potentialities that make man human and make the world and the universe something infinitely more than a very complicated mechanism. Quantitatively man is nothing, he is only very complex. The best he can become is to be found only in the domain of the qualitative.

Science is nevertheless conscientiously sticking to its task of quantifying everything in the name of humanity; but in accepting the claims of science to a superior and even universal authority, humanity is not acting in its own best interests. Science seems to offer much in the way of comfort and convenience, relief from physical suffering and the hope of abundance for all; but it can never do anything to favor the development of the qualities that distinguish man from the animals, nor can it give him a purpose in life other than a search for terrestrial well-being. Science, and the people as well, seem to assume that if terrestrial welfare is looked after, the spirit of man, that is to say the qualitative aspect of man's nature, will look after itself; but that is not so, because the two things, though by no means necessarily incompatible, do not lie in the same direction. We can choose—indeed we cannot avoid choosing—

---

4. Meanwhile, it seeks to 'explain' qualities such as color, coherence, weight, luminosity and so on; and no doubt it would like, if it could, similarly to 'explain' beauty and goodness and greatness and even love itself, much as in its psychological branches it now seeks to 'explain' religion.

The place of religion in the scientific system is treated as a branch of psychology or sociology or anthropology, according to whether the emphasis is on the individual or the group. But in religion beauty and goodness are very much in question, and, more than either, holiness, qualities which the scientific approach is designed to eliminate as far as possible. Holiness in particular, being absolutely undefinable, has no 'scientific' meaning whatever.

which shall be our main direction. It is precisely in this respect that our wills are free. We can look to a terrestrial future in which every man can have all he desires for the asking, and if that seems unattainable we can comfort ourselves by imagining a migration by our remote descendants to another planet. Alternatively, we can look into our own hearts here and now, and consider whether there is not some purpose in life greater than that of the terrestrial welfare of ourselves and our descendants.

We need guidance in our choice, and for the present we have accepted the guidance of science. We have been misled into thinking that man is the measure of all things, and that his very unscientific free will makes it possible for him to mould the world to his desires, provided only that he is scientific enough in other respects. We are told that predestination, in the form of a rigid nexus of ascertainable laws, is the rule in the non-human world.

These two conceptions are not mutually consistent. If either is correct the other is not. We are encouraged to think, not of what we ourselves might be, but of how to mould our environment to our desires. The machine, that characteristic product of science, becomes the instrument of our fulfillment; we devote ourselves to its service and become thereby subject to its dominion. In doing so we drag ourselves down to its level and become more and more mere cogs in a machine. Sometimes we instinctively revolt against this situation, but our revolt is nearly always misdirected because we have no idea of where to look for the real source of our discontent. We dare not look within ourselves. We seek comfort instead in the ever-widening opportunities for distraction afforded by scientific developments. All this could never have happened if the prevailing mentality had not been sufficiently ready to welcome it, if that mentality had not already been sufficiently detached from the realities underlying its own nature and destiny. Modern science and the modern mentality are but one. There is no greater mistake than to assume that human mentality always remains the same or that it always progresses.

Must we then accept our submission to a law that is inexorable but inherently undefinable, a law that cannot be grasped in its entirety yet cannot be escaped?

Something of the kind has been accepted almost universally in the past. All peoples have always believed in some kind of law or power the nature of which they can never hope to comprehend fully, but which is at the same time the ultimate arbiter of their destiny. Scientific man cannot bring himself to admit that his unscientific predecessors, even when they thought that the earth was flat or that the stars were holes in the sky, may have been nearer than he is to an understanding of the nature of the most comprehensive and the most fundamental laws of the universe. These are evidently the laws that count for most; indeed they are exactly the laws which science is most anxious to discover. But, if they are inherently undefinable, the approach of science defeats its own ends.

It is unnecessary to point out that the old approach is, broadly speaking, the approach of religion. The fundamental principle common to all religions is that of the dependence of the universe on something too exalted to be grasped by the senses or by discursive thought and too comprehensive to be escaped.[5] It is not a question of whether science is logical and religion is not, or the other way round, it is a question of the foundations of the logic of each. Given the foundation on which the logic of religion is built up, it is not illogical that the influence of the undefinable should be manifested in a way that eludes the mind of man, nor that all things and all

---

5. The variety of the applications of this principle in no way affect it as a principle, even though some alleged applications may be decadent or even subversive of truth. No more appropriate terms being available, the words 'religion' or 'the religious point of view' are used here with an almost exclusive emphasis on the dependence of religion on the principle in question, without reference to the special characteristics of any particular application, except that false applications are by implication excluded. This may seem to be an oversimplification of a very complex situation; the alternative is an overcomplication which would undoubtedly obscure the main issue. The present aim is only to suggest a firm basis on which the study of those complications can, if necessary, be pursued.

beings should be regarded as subject to its operation, whether they be conscious of the fact or not.

The difference between man and other beings is precisely that he is—or can be—conscious of his own situation in this respect. This power of the human consciousness is proof of its full development. The conception of man's situation formed by an individual or by a group may be true or false in very varying degrees, man being what he is. In any case, man's situation being what it is, an apprehension of its nature can only be direct, intuitive and interior, and not indirect, deductive and exterior. Logic can play a part in reinforcing or clarifying intuition, but cannot procure it where it is not already present or at least latent.

Many people are unable to accept this sort of view, on the grounds that the resulting conceptions are necessarily vague, and that, not being precisely definable, they cannot provide a firm basis for reasoning. Nevertheless, if it be true that reality does not reside within the domain of the quantitative and measurable, but rather in that of the qualitative and non-measurable, then the only sound foundation for reasoning is necessarily a clear intuition, synthetic rather than analytical and more penetrating than mere observation. The resulting conceptions may not be perfect, and they may be communicable only to those who in some degree share the same intuition, but they will be better than conceptions confined to the indefinite cyclical movements of relativity, which themselves offer no way of escape from their own endless concatenation.

The scientific point of view insists that nothing can properly be regarded as intelligible unless or until it can be defined. Religion, at least in its origin and in principle, is opposed to this view, and has a much wider conception of intelligibility. Nowadays the representatives of religion dare not appear to be otherwise than up-to-date. That is why they are always seeking to make the scriptures and doctrines of religion 'intelligible' to the average person by attempting to define them in terms suited to his powers of mental analysis and deduction. It is not those powers that limit anyone's grasp of what religion is about. On the contrary, nothing limits it more surely than a mania for definition, whether philosophical or popular. A definable deity is not divine but human; not God but an idol.

Divinity is intelligible but not definable, and it would not be Divinity if anything or anybody could be independent of its laws. Man is equal to all other beings in his submission, though superior in his degree of consciousness. Being alone fully conscious, he alone can be conscious of his submission

One cannot be conscious of anything save by contrast with what it is not, or with its negation. If we did not know darkness, we should not know light. The awareness of a distinction or of a negation implies the possibility of an inward choice between this and that, between plus and minus. There can be no such possibility in the absence of the awareness, but where the awareness is present the possibility cannot but present itself. Thus man's freedom to choose, relative though it be, is a function of the fact that he alone is fully conscious.

If the privilege accompanying a full development of consciousness is free will, its price is the possibility of self-delusion. The possibility of grasping a situation depends on the possibility of seeing that it is not some other situation. This in its turn carries with it the possibility of imagining situations and confusing them with the real situation. This is what science thinks our forefathers were doing.

The question is: who is in fact living in an imaginary situation, religious man or scientific man? The latter is particularly liable to imagine that his degree of free will is much greater than it really is, up to the point of imagining that he is himself an independent being and master of all he surveys.

There is much talk of a reconciliation of the points of view of religion and science. How can one reconcile two systems of thought that start from mutually contradictory assumptions concerning the nature of reality itself?

One or the other must give way in the end, and it is not difficult to see which is giving way at present. Reconciliation could be effected only by situating the two in their correct hierarchical order.

The subordination of the religious outlook to the scientific has now reached a point at which most people habitually assume that their freedom of choice is limited only by their individual and collective capacity to overcome the natural obstacles they encounter on their 'forward march'. We think much about overcoming those obstacles, but little about becoming ourselves; becoming what we might be. When we do think of that, we think in terms of education or eugenics[6] or the provision of better environmental conditions.

Nothing we impose on ourselves by the exercise of our combined inventiveness and goodwill can do anything to change our hearts, which cannot be changed save by the intervention of something greater than ourselves. We cannot, in the nature of things, procure that intervention, but we can, by the exercise of our free will within the limits assigned to it, either shut the door upon it or open our hearts to it.

We have seen that the reconciliation of the idea of predestination, implicit as it is in the conception of the regulation of the universe by definable laws, with the evident fact of human free will, raises grave difficulties from the scientific point of view. The contemporary religious point of view tends to share those difficulties exactly insofar as it is subordinated to the scientific point of view. If we are to see how they can be resolved in the religious point of view we must go back to the origin of the universe and of man, of which the most familiar account is that given in the Book of Genesis. Incidentally, no part of the Bible has come in for more criticism than Genesis, on the grounds that it is unscientific. But critical analysis and an insistence on unequivocal definition can only hide its real content: and the

---

6. Hence no doubt the idea that it may some day become desirable and possible to breed a 'superman', with faculties more highly developed than those of his makers. There are already techniques, computerized and commercialized, whereby we can produce hens that will lay seventy or more eggs, infertile but edible, every hundred days. Many more far-reaching projects are now in hand or adumbrated, including the production of artificial genes. So why not a superman, even if we have to wait some time? Certain incidental difficulties would have to be overcome, such as that of how to dispose of the many failures inevitable in an experiment of this kind; neither permanent incarceration nor simple murder are attractive alternatives. But if all difficulties could be overcome, what would a superman be like? He would be a failure unless his brain-power were of a much higher order than that of his makers; inevitably therefore they would be unable to follow the workings of his mind, and so would have no means of telling whether they had in fact produced a superman or a madman. Yet, for the same reason, he could subordinate their wills to his. So much is clear, and it is no less clear to anyone who accepts the traditional teachings concerning what man is and what he ought to be that this superman could only be a devil.

same applies to all Sacred Scriptures, for what they are concerned with in the first place is the undefinable.

We read that 'in the beginning God created the heavens and the earth...' and later that He 'created man in His own image and likeness.' If God had not 'created the heavens and the earth,' His Totality would not have been made manifest in multiplicity as well as in unity, in distinction as well as in non-distinction, in contrast as well as in harmony, in personality as well as in non-personality, in time as well as in eternity, in space as well as in infinity. Because such a manifestation is possible, in its absence Totality would have been less than total; any such supposition is nonsensical *ab initio*.

The universe is as it were a reflection of the Totality of its Supreme Cause; but it is a reflection limited and particularized by the characteristics of the mirror in which it is seen, namely, by number, form, time, space, mass and all the other conditions peculiar to our universe. Incidentally, an indefinite number of other sets of conditions and combinations is possible, and with them an indefinite number of universes other than our own.[7] The conceptions of science cover only one aspect or modality even of our own universe, namely, the quantitative. The big mistake resides in treating the quantitative aspect as principal or fundamental. It is our preoccupation with physical measurement that makes the mere size of the physical universe and the smallness of sub-atomic entities so astonishing to us; we are staggered by the contrast and immensely impressed by our own ability to measure it. But if space is indefinite in extent and indefinitely divisible, we can go on indefinitely developing our apparatus and methods without getting any nearer to finality, and more importantly, without getting any nearer to the essential factors of causation that lie outside the visible universe.

---

7. The spiral nebulae are sometimes called 'universes', though in fact they are all within our universe, which we see as 'our universe' because our senses are adapted to the conditions which make it what it is. No universe other than our own can ever be accessible to our senses, but it is absurdly anthropomorphic to suggest that therefore no other universe is possible. We have got into the habit of regarding as real only what is accessible to our senses, and as possible only what can be imagined as coming into the same category. This is the very error against which the present argument is directed.

Even when we attribute—and rightly—all the wonder and beauty of the universe to God, we often forget that the timeless and the spaceless are incomparably more wonderful and more beautiful.[8] The universe did not create itself, and the secret of its creation, being greater than it, cannot be contained by it. That secret can only be grasped intuitively and communicated symbolically, and the symbolism of Genesis is sufficient, though not the only possible symbolism.[9] It emphasizes the apparent separation of the universe from its supreme Cause, and the rest of the Bible shows that this Cause can never cease to be operative, otherwise the universe, having no longer any raison d'être, would cease to exist. The separation of the universe from God can never become complete.

We are told that God put man, made in His own image and likeness, into the world as his representative, lest that separation should become complete.[10] Being made in the image of God man must reflect, however dimly, the attributes of Divinity. Now God is not affected by anything nor changed by anything; having no needs and

---

8. Better than the best the earth can show. A conjunction of the crescent moon with the evening star can be overwhelming in its beauty; as it were a signed guarantee that all is well. This aspect of the event is independent of, and immeasurably more significant than, anything that is known or can be known about either heavenly body. Yet under the implacable eye of science beauty becomes a luxury, goodness a policy, and truth a formula.

9. There is another Biblical 'account of the Creation' in the prelude to the Gospel according to St John. It is very different from the account in Genesis, but this by no means implies that one is right or the other wrong, nor that one is in any way inferior to the other.

10. The function of 'keeping in touch with' God is normally exercised collectively, by way of the spiritual hierarchy on which every civilization worthy of the name is founded, and within which every man has his part, however humble, to play. Such a civilization, whether it be on a small scale or on a big scale, is held together by a chain of personal loyalty to a superior and not by an ideology. The immediate superior is seen as an indispensable link in the chain down which flows the divine Grace. Where no such chain exists or where it has become too rusty, ever-growing confusion is inevitable.

no desires and being utterly free from all ties, He is dependent on nothing. It is this attribute, the attribute of total Independence, that is reflected in human free will. Man is potentially a saint because he is made in the image of God, but also potentially a trouble-maker because he is imperfect and at the same time endowed with free will.

It is very natural to ask the question; 'If God is the Creator, why did He not make mankind wholly subject to His commands, rather than free to disobey them, thus avoiding all the trouble he causes?' This is the very question asked of God by the angels in the Koran, to which God answered, 'I know what you know not'.[11] The situation of beings subject to the limitations of a particular state, whether angelic or human or any other, is necessarily marked by an intrinsic limitation of knowledge or comprehension. The first step towards wisdom is to be aware of this fact, expressed as it is with characteristic conciseness in the sentence quoted. God's answer to the angels is sufficient; but we are always avid for what we can regard as a rational explanation, or an explanation expressed in terms of human values. It is not difficult to satisfy that avidity by reflecting that a world without free will, while it might be less trouble, would also be less potentially good, because its submission to God would not be conscious. Compare a caged animal with one that is free but will come to call for love of its master.

Free will would not be free will if we could not misuse it. It would have no significance if its misuse carried no consequences. If that were the case the principle of causality would be infringed, and that is impossible. When we delude ourselves that we are independent beings, and that the world is ours insofar as we can make it so by the application of our superior mental powers, we are misusing the gift of free will. That gift was given to us in order that we might choose, collectively as well as individually, to put the search for the Holy Grail first and to subordinate to it the search for a formula. The consequences, both individual and collective, of a wrong choice are inescapable. Judgment is not arbitrary, it is in the very nature of things. It is simply the compensation which restores the equilibrium of an order that has been temporarily disturbed.

11. Koran 11:30.

From this point of view predestination and free will are not difficult to reconcile. On the contrary, they appear as essential features of a single whole: for unless the course of events were predestined, in the sense of its being regulated in accordance with a timeless principle, there could be no order, but without human free will that order would not be brought to perfection. The logic behind this view of things can be, and has been, put into words in endless different ways.[12]

Lao Tzu (c. 550 BC) begins his great treatise, the *Tao Te Ching*, thus: 'The way that can be traced is not the Way; the name that can be pronounced is not the Name.'

No science that does not give first place to this truth is worthy so to be called. The measure of man's true humanity lies in his grasp of this truth and in his use of his free will for the ordering of his life in conformity with it.

---

12. None of which can be intrinsically unequivocal, since their object is the incommunicable; moreover it will not look like logic at all to anyone to whom its starting-point is not more or less self-evident. That starting point could be said to be the supreme relevance of the undefinable.

VI

Planning for Progress

The modern obsession with strategic planning is a symptom of an extreme anxiety about the future. This is not unrelated to an extreme lack of trust in God.[1]

Something that can be called 'planning' is of course involved whenever anyone considers what he is going to do next. This is simply the adaptation of the action of the moment to a reasonable anticipation of the future. It is a normal and necessary feature of human life. The new and rather special kind of planning with which modern civilization is obsessed is collective planning on a big scale and having a relatively distant future in view. It is a gigantic exercise in anticipation covering the entire social, political and economic field. Its objectives are a better standard of living, an absence of open conflict and above all progress. Modern strategic planning prides itself on being scientific, and it looks to modern science to supply the means for the realization of its intentions. It is a very different thing from the natural, necessary and often more or less instinctive moment to moment or day to day foresight of the individual or the group. Long-term comprehensive planning seems in these days to offer the only hope of enabling civilization as we know it to implement its own ideals of progress.

Two fundamental assumptions underlie this modern planning; the first is the idea that man is absolute master of his own destiny,

---

1. There are of course still many people who would admit that their destiny and that of the world is in the hands of God and not in the hands of man; nevertheless, such people are usually scarcely less anxious than are people who believe that the future is in the hands of man alone.

and the second is the no less widespread notion that evolution is in some rather ill-defined sense progressive. The agnostic has no reason to question the first, and is all too anxious to ignore any reasons there may be for questioning the second. The believer has every reason to question both, although most believers seem to have lost sight of those reasons.

The difference between the points of view of believers and unbelievers has something absolute about it, but in practice attitudes and motives often seem to be very mixed. The position of believers is much the more difficult because their fundamental beliefs are under constant attack, some of which is calculated and ably directed, while the rest is purely negative and massive. Their belief in God as Creator and Disposer is challenged by the prevailing assumption of man's mastery over his own destiny; their belief in a divine judgment is challenged by the notion of progressive evolution. Anxious not to be called 'reactionary', they are always trying to reconcile religion with contemporary ideas. Perhaps that is why we sometimes hear God's ordering of the universe spoken of as 'God's plan', as if it were analogous to a human plan. If it were, it would be provisional and changeable and restricted to the conditions of terrestrial experience, whereas God's dispositions are immutable and transcendent, otherwise God is not God.

It therefore behoves all who profess a belief in God to plan—as sometimes they must—with as much understanding of God's dispositions as they can achieve, and with a mind open to His guidance. Then, and only then, can their plans rest on a foundation consistent with their beliefs.

In a sense the nature of God's dispositions is self-evident and beyond all doubt. They must include everything that has been or is or will be, and exclude everything that has not been or is not or will not be; otherwise God is not God, Creator, All-knowing, All-powerful and Changeless. Nothing can be outside or contrary to His dispositions; they are manifested in everything, including in ourselves, and in everything we are or do. We can in no sense insulate ourselves from them in the smallest particular, still less can we influence them in any way.

'God's plan' is not like a human plan, and it is directed to ends that may not coincide with those of most human plans, or with human desires. We can come nearer to an understanding of it if, instead of making a god in our own image, we contemplate what we call the 'laws of Nature'. They are as it were the reflection in terms of time, space and other terrestrial conditions of God's immutable and all-embracing dispositions. We can look upon those laws as a whole, and in all their diversity—not slurring over the parts we do not like—as an exposition in time-space language of timeless and ubiquitous Divine principles. We can never know those principles as they are 'in themselves', but only 'as in a glass, darkly'. Yet we must not forget that those Divine principles are the origin and end of all things known and unknown and must therefore be acknowledged as such in principle and in practice.

Alternatively we can adopt the modern outlook and look upon those laws of nature as no more than so many independent facts of observation which can only be seen as a whole insofar as we can form a mental picture of their observable relationships, and thereby formulate more comprehensive laws by a process of comparison and deduction.

The choice of starting-point is ours, and because we are fallible either choice can lead to error. The second choice however has error as its starting-point, because it treats phenomena as the fundamental reality. It alone necessarily leads in the end to delusion.

If we can in no way be exempted from God's dispositions, even the possibility of human delusion must itself be a part of those dispositions, and must be taken into account accordingly. In fact, it is that possibility alone which introduces an element of doubt into our understanding of God's dispositions, thereby blurring their self-evidence and bringing them within the range of discussion, but by no means within the range of any conclusive formulation or verbal description.

No error is more fatal in the end than that of deciding that, simply because we cannot fathom the mystery, or because every image of God is inevitably inadequate, we can or must proceed as if we were independent of God. A sufficient humility before God is a precondition of understanding: 'The fear of the Lord is the beginning of wisdom.'[2]

2. Ps. 3:10.

This implies an attitude of mind far removed from that which seems to underlie most modern large-scale planning, dominated as it is by the assumption that the future of man depends entirely on his own good intentions together with his ingenuity in dealing with a blind and hostile environment. Many people who share that attitude of mind feel that they need not despair, even in face of the knowledge that some day the earth will be involved in a cataclysm which will make life as we know it impossible. They believe that evolutionary progress is a law of Nature, and that the men of the future may therefore be expected to have gained powers unknown and scarcely imaginable to the man of today, and that those powers will enable them to predict and to cope with all possible emergencies. This is the only alternative to a philosophy of despair. It is quite evident that no such ideas can be found in the scriptures or the traditions of any religion, despite the fact that some ingenious thinkers—notably Teilhard de Chardin—have contrived to graft them on to their own interpretation of religion.

Such distortions of religion do not alter the fact that religion and science envisage the origin and destiny of the universe and of mankind in two different ways, and that those two ways are in principle mutually exclusive. Religion envisages the origin and destiny of the universe and of mankind as supernatural and therefore not observable; science envisages it as natural and in principle observable. In these days the outlook of science has colored or replaced that of religion to such an extent that the difference of principle has been largely obscured. This state of affairs is conspicuously exemplified in the fact that almost everyone, believers and unbelievers alike, accepts the validity of the theories of progressive evolution developed in the recent past. In accordance with these theories, human history is conceived as being part of an evolutionary process, beginning at a remote point in time, and thereafter 'progressive' in general tendency, despite the fairly regular occurrence of reversals or relapses. Progress in this sense is conceived as a process of change leading from a 'primitive' to an 'advanced' state, the latter being characterized by wealth, culture and freedom from pain and fear. The realization of this advanced state is assumed to be a continuous process, occasional delays being compensated by periods of acceleration. Since modern science is seen to represent *ex hypothesis* an advance on earlier wisdoms, it will play a major part in that realization, its destructive power being turned to peaceful ends. Such is the basis of the hopes that are nowadays shared in a large measure by believers and unbelievers alike. Strategic plans are shaped accordingly.

Christianity is the dominant religion in the West, and in the West the idea of an evolutionary progress was first formulated. The impact of those theories on Christianity in particular is emphasized here, partly because the Christian religion and tradition have borne the brunt of the attack, and partly because they are likely to be more familiar to readers than any others.³ Most of what is said here is however applicable, *mutatis mutandis*, to non-Christian countries and peoples, for the state of affairs is now broadly speaking the same all over the world. Religion and tradition as a whole are under attack; perhaps in the end that attack may be of service in revealing the transcendent Unity that underlies the diversity in the outward forms of religions.⁴

The expectation of a progress of the kind briefly outlined above is so pervasive that the Christian promise seems often to be interpreted in that sense alone. Consequently, for some Christians at least, any other anticipation would represent a contradiction of the Christian hope, and even something like a denial of faith in the goodness of God. The events that must, according to the Scriptures, precede the fulfillment of the Christian promise are accordingly glossed over or thrust into the background as far as possible.

The Scriptures foresee a period of decadence followed by a judgment of great severity and comprehensiveness, and only thereafter

---

3. Specific reference to other religions and traditions would involve unessential complications and reservations.

4. See *The Transcendent Unity of Religions* by Frithjof Schuon (London: Faber and Faber, 1953).

will there be 'a new heaven and a new earth';[5] this clearly implies a new religion and a new humanity, not a reformed religion and the same humanity. There will be as it were a discontinuity in history; there will be 'time no longer'.[6] When this great judgment comes, it will doubtless not be recognized as such, but only as a great disaster. The world will blame anything and everything but itself. Even religion will no doubt be blamed, as it is today in many quarters on the grounds that it is a hindrance to progress.

Predictions concerning the end of the world are nothing new nor are they peculiar to religion. Only those that come directly from sacred Scripture or tradition can properly be called 'prophecies', because they enunciate principles rather than predicting the course of events. The principles they enunciate are of universal application at all levels. They can therefore be related not only to 'judgments' that are cosmic in scale, but also to those that are more or less localized or even internal and individual. There are many 'worlds' in the wide sense of the word: not only this earth, but also every subdivision of its living envelope that has a distinctive life and character, for instance every religion, every civilization and every human individual—since each of us lives in a world of his own. Every 'world', great or small, must have an end because it had a beginning.

The world in which we live is supremely important to the present humanity, for whom it is *the* world, but it is by no means the only possible world. Since at present we know no other, scriptural prophecies are for us related to the beginning and the end of our world, or to the beginning and the end of the more important phases of its history. Ideas such as these are totally incompatible with the supposedly scientific conception of a continuous evolution.

To an unprejudiced mind it must be evident that the course of Nature, the course of history, the whole process of existence, consists

---

5. Rev. 21:1

6. Rev. 10:6. — The advent of each of the great Revelations represents a discontinuity comparable in kind but on a less comprehensive scale, for they too are interruptions of the 'natural' course of history by an irruption of the 'supernatural', and they too are always preceded by a period of spiritual decadence in the civilization of their origin.

in a perpetual appearance, growth, decay and disappearance of things distinguished from other things by their forms, whether they be cosmic or terrestrial, collective or individual, material or psychic or, like life itself, both at once.[7]

Scientific man knows deductively that the world must come to an end; yet he tries to plan the physical survival of the human race, and meanwhile he lives for the sensation of the moment.

Traditional man is made aware of the same truth by revelation; but it does not occur to him to plan for an indefinite physical survival, because he has something better than the sensation of the moment to live for—and to die for.

The truth that is represented is in both cases the same; the difference between them is that the scientific representation of that truth lacks an essential dimension, or rather, *the* essential dimension.

All human institutions have a distinctive form, and are therefore perishable. Religion, insofar as it is a human institution, is no exception. Its essence alone is imperishable, but its essence is formless. Christians are taught to believe that in the end the world will be Christianized, and that this is what the coming of the Kingdom of God means. This is true only in the sense that the essence of Christianity is universal and imperishable, and that the world cannot live without it; but it is untrue insofar as it is held to imply that the distinctive beliefs and formal observances of Christianity must become world-wide. Hence, an incomprehension on the part of Christians of the present state of Christianity as a human institution, and their frequent discouragement. It is not the principles of Christianity that have changed, only men have changed.

---

7. The universality of this law of impermanence compels scientists, in their search for an observable ultimate cause, to constantly try to extend the limits of the observable in the direction of the very small or the very great. It is not surprising that the main results of their efforts have so far been to reveal the impermanence of the atom and the cataclysmic nature of phenomena on the cosmic scale. They cannot deny that an end of this world in a purely physical sense is inevitable, though it may be long deferred in relation to our usual terrestrial time-scale. The fact that everything that possesses a distinctive form, and is therefore in principle observable, began at a point in time and will end at another represents no new idea, in religion, in philosophy or in science.

The greatest mistake Christians can make is to allow incomprehension or disappointment to weaken their faith. The spirit, the formless essence, is always there, and it will show itself to whoever seeks it uncritically and unreservedly.

How can Christians do otherwise than believe that all things come from God and are sustained by Him and must return to Him? And so it is with the followers of other religions, though they may express this fundamental certainty in very different ways, for this truth is not so narrow that it can be formulated in only one way, or approached from only one direction. Anyone, however, whether he be a Christian or not, can fall into error by misinterpreting this truth or limiting its applications. Anyone may construct for himself a picture of reality which is inconsistent with this fundamental certainty. Such, evidently, is any picture based on the conception of a continuous linear 'progress', of which the end is by definition different from or better than the beginning.

The God to whom all things return is not different from the God from whom they came. The beginning and the end are the same. The journey between them is therefore a cycle and not a progress.

The existence of all things must conform to this pattern; all things have a beginning and an end, and the end is a return to the beginning. Thus the true picture is one of a rhythmical and infinitely complex interlacement of cycles, at every level and on every scale, cosmic, terrestrial and individual, and not one of a unidirectional tendency. As a conception it is very much more difficult to grasp than that of a continuous movement in one direction, but if the former is true and the latter false, considerations of difficulty are beside the point.

All the celestial, terrestrial and biological cycles so familiar to us exemplify the rhythmical principle that underlies and governs all existence: the movements of the heavenly bodies and their periodic changes; the alternations of the seasons, of the months and of day and night, birth and death, the appearance and disappearance of species, the rise and fall of empires, the endless repetition of bud, flower, seed and fruit, the waves of the sea; our heart-beats and our breathing; all these and endless other familiar things are effectual symbols of this rhythmical principle.

Scientific man does not see them as symbols, but merely as phenomena; he therefore misses their power to suggest, each in its own way, some aspect of the mystery of existence, something infinitely greater than itself. The scientific method tries to link phenomena together by physical or mental chains, but in reality there is nothing that holds them together except the Unity from which they sprang and to which they must return. They are relative and differentiated, whereas that 'Unity' is absolute and undifferentiated. It is thus not identifiable with or comparable to any of its productions; it is the ultimate mystery, at once infinitely far and infinitely near.

Many scientists admit that the ultimate must always be mysterious, but they seem to prefer to leave the matter in abeyance on the grounds that we can do nothing about it—yet we are the only creatures who can do anything about it. The ultimate is indeed outside the purview of science, and so people who think that the findings of science represent as nearly as possible the ultimate truth can hardly do otherwise than treat mystery as irrelevant. In doing so they reject, in fact if not in intention, not only mystery but reality itself.

Reality—which in this connection is synonymous with truth—resides in that which is total and eternal and therefore unspecifiable, while at the same time it is inescapable, since we ourselves and everything we know are no more than fragmented reflections of it.

Our whole life is nothing but movement and change, within and without. Yet believers say that God is changeless, eternal, infinite and absolute. The reconciliation of existence with God is therefore a reconciliation of time with eternity, of space with infinity and of relativity with the absolute. Eternity is never absent, it is never not now; nevertheless, it is not wrong to situate it for practical purposes in the future, as we do when we speak of a 'hereafter'. To do so brings the truth as nearly as it can be brought to us while we are tied to time which, from our point of view, is uni-directional. From the 'point of view of eternity', which is not ours as creatures, time is swallowed up in an 'eternal present' and becomes nothing. Similarly, from the 'point of view of infinity' space becomes nothing, and from 'the point of view of the absolute' relativity becomes nothing. And from the 'point of view' of That which has no name—call It totality or non-duality if you will—even eternity, infinity and absoluteness, insofar as they differ one from the other, are not more than particularized reflections of Itself in the mirror of our minds, and so 'less real' than It is in Itself. But these are only words, inevitably inadequate, and that is why some of them are put in inverted commas.

The mystery of existence is really a mystery, and not merely a problem, and so it will be for as long as humanity endures. Nevertheless, the situation can be envisaged in a manner that is at least far less erroneous than that associated with progressive evolutionary theories. One can consider the ceaseless movements of existence as governed by two opposite tendencies, one towards separation from the eternal reality that is its origin, and the other towards a return to that reality. Since the world cannot stand still, the interaction of these two tendencies is expressed in a rhythmical alternation between the two. Thus decadence, a 'falling away' from reality towards an imagined self-sufficiency, is inevitable, but it is necessarily followed by renewal. No other view of things fits in so well with the observable characteristics and history of the world in which we live; no other view of things makes sense of the world as we know it; and no other view of things can make comprehensible to us what may be called, with all due reservations, 'God's plan'.

By contrast, according to the evolutionary or scientific point of view, the advent of Christianity (or of any religion considered to be the vehicle of a Divine Revelation) is seen as representing no more than a step, though a critical one, in a more or less continuous process of change, leading from a rudimentary state towards a perfection that must always be only relative, otherwise evolution would have come to an end. No absolute criterion of that relative perfection can be suggested. A scientific philosophy can only envisage it in terms of what may broadly be called the power of self-determination of the human race, its expertise in planning. According to this view, the future is always nearer than the past to some kind of terrestrial utopia, which is attainable only through the development of that power of self-determination. Christianity (or religion) can only be seen as a factor of historical importance in that development. Therefore religion is expected to exemplify the law of progress. This implies that in its earlier stages religion must have been 'primitive', in the sense of being undeveloped and to that extent incomplete; and that its later manifestations or interpretations are then likely to be superior to the earlier; and moreover their superiority must be measurable in terms of conformity to contemporary ideas, which are *ex hypothesi* believed to be superior to earlier ideas.

The traditional point of view sees Revelation as an irruption of the timeless into time, bringing humanity back in full circle to its timeless origin and thereby reminding it of its destiny. The manifestation of Christianity in time is therefore necessarily anticipated by all that precedes it, fully contemporary at any moment of time, and fulfilled by all that follows it. Christianity is in the world and it has therefore a distinctive form which, as such, is necessarily exclusive of other forms and perishable, but it is also 'not of this world',[8] supra-formal and therefore neither exclusive of other forms nor perishable; containing all truth and expressing it in its own unique way, and thus potentially an enrichment of all true religion, past, present and future, and only provisionally and for purely temporary reasons a denial or a replacement; able to communicate to 'him that hath ears to hear' all that is necessary for salvation, while providentially adapted to the needs of its times, that is to say, to its situation in a cycle of which it is a necessary part; and doubtless perpetually to be renewed in forms similarly adapted to temporal needs in other cycles. It is perfection manifested in imperfection. But imperfection cannot 'know' perfection, and is therefore disinclined to 'receive' it.[9]

Is not Christianity seen in some such way something greater, more wonderful, more evidently a manifestation of eternal truth, more profound, more all-embracing than it is when seen as an incident, even one of the highest significance, in a 'progress' the very notion of which implies that it can, and indeed must, be improved on in due course? Certain modernist movements inside the Churches seem to think they are improving Christianity. But if

---

8. John 18:36
9. John 1:10–11.

Christianity was not perfect at its origin, whence come its virtue and its power? Certainly not from anything that has happened subsequently. That, surely, is the very foundation of the Christian faith?

If the virtue and power of Christianity seem to have waned, at least in their outward manifestations, their restoration can only come by way of a return to the origin, and by no means by way of any kind of 'reformation' which aims to change the very content of Christianity by adapting it to a point of view claiming an absolute superiority over all earlier points of view.

It will be said: but surely mankind has progressed through the ages despite all ups and downs? What about the paleontological evidence?... and so on. The assessment of the position in that respect depends on three main considerations. Firstly, the fact that historical time, and even paleontological time, constitutes but a fraction of what may be called an 'aeon' or major cycle. Every cycle, great or small, comprises a phase or phases that can be regarded as progressive from one point of view or another. A concentration of attention on one such phase, and the projection of its characteristics into time as a whole, is an error. Secondly, it is always tempting to anyone who believes in progress to consider as primitive tendencies that are in reality merely decadent. Thirdly, and even more importantly, everything depends on the point of view from which any particular tendency is labeled as progressive. If the criteria of progress are the increase of wealth and the variety of sensorial experience attainable during life, the answer will be one thing; but if the supreme criterion—not so much of progress as of value—is the nearness of man to God, the answer will be quite another. This supreme criterion is very difficult to assess in past civilizations, because it leaves but few traces. Sometimes there are traces in the form of signs or symbols, the appreciation of which demands a sympathy not procurable by academic study alone. If so many people today fail to understand the symbolism of that model of the universe, the Cross, how can we expect them to understand an alien symbolism from the distant past?

⊕

The greater part of this chapter has been devoted to a statement of some of the more important principles underlying the traditional outlook; partly because they have become relatively unfamiliar to so many people, but also in order to show that the picture of reality associated with the traditional outlook, while it is not incompatible with a proper degree of foresight in human affairs, nevertheless offers a background to any kind of planning very different from that which seems to lie behind most contemporary planning.[10]

It is given to the human race alone to use its intelligence in such a way as to enable it to exercise foresight in its activities. It cannot therefore be wrong in principle that we should make use of our unique prerogative. Yet at the same time the Gospels tell us to 'take no thought for the morrow.'[11] How can we reconcile these apparent contraries? We can only begin to do so if in the first place we acknowledge to the full the submission of the human will to the Will of God, if every thought for the future is accompanied by a '*Deo volente*'. *This* by itself can teach us not to worry about the future, even when conditions may seem to make it impossible not to think about it.

The whole matter has another and less contingent aspect. We cannot act in the future any more than we can act in the past; we can act only in the present. Too much concern for the future can only lead us away from the Presence of God here and now, for God is Eternal and therefore for us while we live His Presence is never not now.

---

10. And if the latter background is illusory, what is the outcome of that planning likely to be? It seems to us that planning is vital to progress, that everything would collapse in ruins if we relaxed our efforts in planning. We think so because we have decided by an overwhelming majority to rely on ourselves and not on God. Perhaps that is why so much modern planning looks like a desperate attempt to escape from a confusion arising from causes that are unperceived, or as a scramble to stop up the gaps in the structure of civilization through which disruptive influences continually obtrude themselves to spoil the image of progress.

11. Matt. 6:25. The Revised Version reads 'Take no thought for your life.'

VII
A Glance at Agriculture

The crust of this earth periodically undergoes upheavals of various kinds and on various scales. In the course of the bigger ones, continents are submerged and new continents are raised up. In between there may be ice-ages, and ages of rain and of warmth affecting the whole surface of the globe, or parts of it only. All such occurrences, gigantic and overwhelming as they are from our point of view, are trivial incidents in a continuous series of changes occurring on a cosmic scale, staggering our imagination by their immensity and their duration, and reducing all terrestrial phenomena to a quantitative insignificance. Quantitatively speaking, human life is doubly insignificant, for it plays so small a part even in the geophysical history of this planet, and this planet cannot be considered as if it were isolated from the solar system, nor as if the solar system were isolated from the rest of the universe.

Therefore, if human life has any significance at all, it is not in the domain of quantity but in the domain of quality. It can only be worth preserving in virtue of its qualitative content or potentiality, although it does have an inherent quantitative aspect, and this cannot be preserved unless its quantitative requirements are met. The satisfaction of those requirements is justified only insofar as it is necessary for the development of the qualitative potentialities of mankind.

The main difficulty that arises in following up this statement is that the nature of those qualitative potentialities cannot be precisely defined. Quantity alone is measurable, quality as such is nameable but not measurable. Quality is forever what it is, and it is either perceived for what it is or not perceived at all. Nothing can convey its nature to anyone who cannot perceive it directly. Yet one must talk about quality, for it is the key to everything; without it there is nothing but the chaos of indistinction, the abstractness of pure number.

In discussing quality, the most that one can do is to compare things that possess a quality with things that do not. Even then the comparison is meaningful only to someone who knows from experience what the quality in question is.

Of no quality is this more true than of the quality, or qualities, that can be called 'spiritual'. The word spiritual is inevitably misapplied or misunderstood by anyone for whom the limits of reality coincide with the limits of the measurable. The measurable is in the last analysis everything that can be brought within the analytical and descriptive powers of the human brain. If there were nothing that transcends those powers, all quality could be in principle reduced to quantity. The essential qualitative distinctiveness of man resides in his spiritual potentialities.

Terrestrial upheavals involve the periodical destruction of lives, human and other. This is apt to strike us as very terrible, and to make it difficult for us to understand how an all-merciful God can have ordered matters so. We forget that the law of birth and death is applicable, not to individual living creatures alone, but to everything on which an association with quantity confers a form, from universes downwards. All must perish; the Spirit, which is pure quality, alone is imperishable and always wholly itself. Both as individuals and as human societies we are perishable. Man has always known this, but at the same time he has always seen that there must, so to speak, be something behind it all, something imperishable and greater than himself.[1] To accept the perishability and dependence of ourselves and of the entire universe of forms, with all the humility that this acceptance implies, is a necessary prelude to the

---

1. If that were not so, both he himself and the perishable world of forms would be wholly unreal, a mere fleeting illusion, causeless and aimless. Not only is any such conception contradicted by our own consciousness of existence, but it is also probably in the last analysis devoid of meaning.

understanding of our situation, and such an understanding is indispensable to effective action. It seems that for the present our achievements in the domain of the quantitative and perishable have obscured from us our dependence on the qualitative and imperishable, thus confusing our sense of direction and frustrating much well-intentioned action.

What has all this to do with agriculture? Everything really; for the double reason that the soil, which is a product of terrestrial upheavals, provides its physical foundation, and that the relation of quality to quantity, not only in the final products of agriculture, but also in our approach to its problems, touches every one of us more closely than most people realize.

From the point of view of biology and economics alone, agriculture is the foundation of human life on this planet, and it has been so ever since the growth of population outstripped the food-producing potentialities of virgin Nature. Once established, it becomes the main expression of the relationship between man and Nature. All other human activities are as it were outgrowths arising from it and are dependent on it. We could get on without them, but not without agriculture. It therefore affects us more directly and more nearly than any other activity; the quality of our lives and our outlook is reflected in it, and its quality is in turn reflected back on them.

This self-evident truth has tended to become overshadowed by the attractions and disturbances of industrial development, but it is now being forced on us again in its quantitative aspect by the rapid increase in world population. Such an increase always seems to accompany an industrial revolution.[2] In an incredibly short time,

---

2. A population explosion is not necessarily or solely a result of more or better food, housing or medical attention, all of which were for instance conspicuously lacking in the earlier stages of the British industrial revolution. They can no doubt help to keep it going once it has started, but they are not its cause.

industrial progress has become the aim of almost all nations, and an aim once established is not readily abandoned, especially when wealth is its target and seems within its grasp. Although we are faced with a danger of world starvation within a few decades, we continue to devote an ever-growing proportion of our money and energies to developments in the industrial field, the demands of which are insatiable. Industry is continually putting out fresh outgrowths which create new opportunities but with them new desires and new needs.[3]

The dominant consideration in industry, the very principle on which it is founded, the consideration to which all others must give way, is the progressive reduction in the financial cost of producing and selling any given article. The purpose of that reduction is to free resources, both human and physical, for the production of a yet wider range of articles. The process is inherently cumulative and accelerative. It implies continual change of a kind that would nowadays be called a 'redeployment of resources'. It also necessitates an unremitting stimulation of the demand for goods, in other words, of desire. It is a case of continually persuading people to want what they did not know they wanted. It would be difficult to invent an economic background less well adapted than this to the fulfillment of the vital functions of agriculture.

As the industrial outlook becomes ever more universal, it becomes increasingly difficult, and eventually impossible, for agriculture to retain an outlook and methods incompatible with those of industry. Agriculture is affected above all by the unceasing worldwide pressure to reduce unit costs by adopting new methods, showing only marginal financial advantages, and continually being superseded by yet newer methods. The resulting instability does nothing but harm. Agriculture adopts the industrial outlook as

---

3. Curiously enough—or perhaps it is not curious at all—the newest desires are at the same time the most expensive and the most absurd, for instance, color television, ever faster travel and putting men on to the moon. Expansion for its own sake is the watchword; it can be achieved most quickly only at someone else's expense; when everyone is aiming at it, rivalry between sectional interests, national or otherwise, is everywhere exacerbated, and preparations for war, whether 'cold' or 'hot', become the biggest drain on resources of all.

nearly as its circumstances permit. It resisted for a long time, but is now thoroughly involved.

The typical organization of settled agriculture has been until recently of the kind known as a peasantry; it disappeared perhaps sooner in Britain than in most other countries. Its essential features are relatively small economic units, usually worked by families who derive most of their sustenance from their own holdings and sell or exchange only their surplus. Each unit or group of units is more or less self-contained and self-supporting both economically and biologically. The techniques of cultivation and care of animals are handed down with little alteration from generation to generation. Within this type of framework many variations can be found and have been studied; some of them have survived here and there to the present day, though not without modification. The way of life of a peasantry is above all traditional; its resistance to change has in the past been perhaps the main stabilizing factor in human civilization, while at the same time it has been a breeding ground of fine human qualities. Even today, among the few survivors of the ancient peasantries, it is possible to find outstanding examples of dignity, poise, and pride of function joined to real craftsmanship, no doubt related to a real sense of the place of man in Nature, and therewith of his relation to God. These qualities can make up for many faults. They are not sufficiently appreciated in these days, for they are not money-spinners; but civilization is nevertheless seriously impoverished when they are rare. The peasant has always been the butt of the smart townsman, although his way of life has also been romanticized. There is no justification for disparagement of the function of the peasant which is indispensable in a settled people.

Insofar as a peasantry retains some vestiges of the Edenic state from which it sprang, that function is much more than simple food-production, since it is the function through which man is integrated with his environment. Its romantic aspect is closely associated with that origin. In its decadence very little of that origin remains.

The peasant way of life has by now almost been wiped off the map of the world. It is true enough that it cannot meet what people perceive as the needs of our times, but then the people of our times do not know what their real needs are. If a peasantry can preserve something that conforms to the most profound human needs, that would at least explain why, of all the forms of human society, it is the most tenacious of life. But even where it has hung on up to the present day, it seems to be doomed. The tractor is replacing the draft animal, electricity is everywhere, television is in the living room and a motor car is in the stall of the beast of burden. In many places where, in spite of all, something of the ancient spirit might survive a little longer, tourism is swamping it with artificiality.

The European and Asian peasant, who is evidently in mind here, is taken as the typical representative of a traditional agriculture. The way of life of the hunting nomad is by definition minimally agricultural, and is therefore excluded from the present discussion, except in order to mention that the true nomad may in many respects often be even nearer to the Edenic state than the peasant, and that the advent of modernism has destroyed his way of life even more quickly and more completely.

It may be worthwhile to summarize the nature of the outward changes brought about in agriculture by the rise to dominance of the modern industrial outlook.

Firstly: a progressive reduction in the number of persons directly engaged in agriculture, both in relation to the volume of its products and to the non-agricultural population. This tendency has gone further in Great Britain and the United States than elsewhere and the proportion of agricultural to total population is still falling. This has been made possible by the mechanization of an ever increasing number of agricultural processes and tasks, including the care of animals. Mechanization is the most typical feature of industrialization in all its forms. It is usually accompanied by the substitution of the wage-earner for the worker having a proprietary interest.

Secondly: and arising directly from the above: progressive increase in the average size of farms and of fields, so that the cost of elaborate and expensive machinery and equipment may be spread over a large area, and so that its use to full capacity may be as far as possible unrestricted. Consequential changes related to systems of tenure, finance, etc., need not be considered here, important though they be.

Thirdly: the substitution of chemical methods for older methods, both for the maintenance of the productivity of the soil and for combating diseases, weeds and pests.

Fourthly: and arising directly out of the three changes already outlined: a progressive loss of economic independence, both in the individual agricultural unit and in agriculture as a whole. Agriculture is already very much dependent on industry for the fulfillment of its functions, and even, particularly in England, on the industry and products of distant lands. Herein lurks a risk of famine so far largely unrecognized.[4]

Fifthly: a growing demand for the standardization of agricultural and horticultural products, to meet the requirements of a mainly urban population, and of the distributors who not only serve it but also persuade it to want what it suits them to offer, namely products that are uniform, well packed in standard quantities and as nearly as possible imperishable. A consequence of all this is the widespread practice of adding preservatives to a growing range of foods.[5] Once again, cheapness is the supposed justification of such practices, but even that advantage can be more than neutralized by costs of

---

4. For instance, British agriculture today is absolutely dependent on machinery, together with supplies of the necessary spare parts, fuel oils, lubricants, electricity and other requirements, many of which come from abroad. Intensive stock farming on modern lines would be impossible without protective and curative drugs and supplements to natural foods; and, for so long as existing economic pressures continue, present-day standards of crop production could not be approached without a liberal use of chemical fertilizers and weed-killers. It has been calculated that to keep one man employed full-time in agriculture in Britain, two men must be employed full-time in industry.

5. The materials used have usually been shown by short-term experiments to be harmless, but, to say the least of it, we are entitled to expect from our food something better than harmlessness.

processing, packing and distribution. There is an ever-growing gap between primary producer and ultimate consumer, conspicuous in its financial aspect although less so in its more important biological aspect. This, of course, is a very big question, covering as it does the whole field of human nutrition.

Sixthly: a growing instability arising out of the increasing rapidity with which the new ideas produced by research, together with economic and political changes, necessitate the adjustment or alteration of methods and of the approach to current problems. Agriculture ceases to be the main stabilizing factor, either economic or social, in a civilization, and finds itself involved willy-nilly in what is commonly called the 'rat-race'.[6] It is perhaps not too wild a guess to say that there has been more change in the past hundred years than in the previous thousand, and more in the last twenty than in the previous two hundred. This acceleration shows no sign of slackening.

All these changes mark the abandonment of a traditional approach in favor of an industrial approach. Industrial progress is founded on modern science, and so it is not surprising that agriculture claims to be more and more scientific, and to a large extent lives up to its claim. Most farmers accept this situation and many even welcome it, for they are far from being immune to infection by the ideology of industrial progress. By them as by others every step in this progress is hailed as an advance, and so it is from the purely industrial point of view. Every innovation brings at least a potential financial gain, but it is necessarily obtained at a price. The only motivation of industry is gain that can be measured in financial terms, but in agriculture the price may have to be paid in a less measurable currency, one that is qualitative rather than quantitative. No instance could be more self-evident than that of the sacrifice of beauty associated with industrial development, including the development of agriculture on industrial lines; a loss not only of natural beauty, but also of beauty in the things man makes for his use or pleasure. This is one of the qualitative losses that has not passed unnoticed. It is regretted, and many attempts are made to

6. It has been described as 'doing unto others before they do unto you.'

100 *Looking Back on Progress*

minimize it, but little is done to attack or even to understand its cause.

There are other problems. For instance, there has been a considerable outcry raised against what is called 'factory farming' as applied to animals, mainly on the grounds that it is cruel, and there has been much argument on both sides. Without going into that argument, it can be asserted with confidence that so long as any producer who can cut his costs while still producing a saleable article can squeeze a producer who cannot do so out of business, there will be 'factory farming' or something very like it, with all its inevitable effects on the quality of its products and on the animals involved.

There is also a controversy about the quality of food grown by 'natural' as against 'artificial' methods. It is really a question, not of natural against artificial, but of the degree of artificiality, the only natural foods being those that are produced in nature without human assistance; but questions of degree can be crucial. The subject can be argued *ad nauseam* and any answer arrived at is sure to be liable to criticism as being a result of prejudice, since no scientific proof is ever likely to be possible. Nothing less than experiments with whole communities prolonged over several generations could provide anything that could be called scientific proof, and by then it would be too late to be of much use.[7]

A return to older methods of cultivation and fertilization does not by itself touch the root of the matter. This does not imply that it may not be worthwhile for its own sake, provided that too much is not expected of it. A few people have tried and are still trying to produce food without the help of chemical fertilizers and sprays, and a few people—perhaps a growing number—prefer to buy food thus produced. Who dares to say that they are wrong? A large majority of people are not interested and much prefer to swim with the stream, and to dismiss the objectors to food grown by modern methods as being mere faddists.

---

7. Studies of living populations can however he informative. See, for example, *The Wheel of Health* by Dr G.T. Wrench (New York: Schocken Books, 1972), a study of the Hunza people of N.W. India, and *Farmers of Forty Centuries* by F.H. King, (Emmaus, PA: Rodale Press, 1973), a study of the Chinese peasantries.

New techniques are adopted by farmers because they know that if they do not keep up to date they will be squeezed out of business. Modern farming has become much more a business than a way of life. The pressure towards an ever more complete industrialization of agriculture is still growing. Farmers are officially encouraged to expect nothing less, in Britain, where certain minimum prices are fixed by the Government, farmers are told that these prices will be based on an expected increase of so much per cent per annum in their 'efficiency', and the measure of that efficiency is exclusively financial. That is why most of the few farms trying in one way or another to fight against contemporary trends have already been squeezed out. They have found out that what was economically possible yesterday is not so today, and will be less so tomorrow.[8]

One thing is abundantly clear. It is unlikely that the growing population of the world can be fed at all in the future otherwise than by the employment of modern scientific agricultural techniques. For it to be fed without using those techniques, a condition would be the abolition of all the quantitative and sentimental ideals of modern civilization and the desires they engender, and the recovery of a sympathy with and an understanding of Nature now in abeyance. It is undeniable that very dense populations have fed themselves for long periods without modern techniques,[9] but their approach to life and its problems and their sense of values were so different from ours that we cannot as a society even understand them, let alone live as they did.

Wherever the line that divides the artificial from the natural may be drawn, their separation has now reached a point at which one can say that the agricultural revolution which has followed on the

---

8. If anyone wants to protect himself from contemporary trends and influences which he believes to be pernicious by growing his own food on his own land in his own way, as he has a perfect right to do, he will get no help and little sympathy. He must be in a position to face an economic isolation which is in practice extremely difficult to realize. It is even more difficult to realize an isolation from the influence of modern civilization in other domains, yet, unless this can be done, the purpose of an economic isolation will be only very partially fulfilled.

9. See note 7. The works referred to are equally informative in connection with the feeding of large populations from small areas of workable land.

heels of the industrial revolution has brought about something like a divorce between man and Nature. Formerly, man lived more or less in harmony with Nature, and played his part in maintaining what we call a 'balance of Nature'. That natural balance, if we could but see it so, represents a fulfillment of the divine ordinances whereby all living things are related one to another through their common origin in God, and those ordinances have both a gentle and a rigorous aspect, a fact which modern sentimentality refuses to recognize.[10] From the modern point of view, ancient man was 'superstitious', meaning that his motives appear often to have been other than purely rational. No account is taken of the fact that those motives may have been in origin super-rational; that agriculture—in common with all other human activities, social, artistic, military and so forth—can ever have been sacred. We often describe it as having been traditional. The words 'sacred' and 'traditional' are, or ought to be, very close together in meaning; today both have come to be more or less assimilated in meaning to the word 'superstitious', which properly speaking is applicable to things that have lost their virtue through the loss of their attachment to their divine origin. The ancient practices cannot be understood in purely economic terms; and when no other terms are regarded as seriously significant, they cannot be understood at all.[11]

10. When we speak disparagingly of the 'law of the jungle' we are looking only at the rigorous aspect of the divine ordinances. It is undeniable that wild animals are liable to misfortunes which sometimes appear to us to be cruel and even unnecessarily so, but it is doubtful whether they are any worse than those to which humanity is liable, more particularly because human troubles are so much more varied, subtle and persistent. It is evident to the most casual observation that wild animals seem almost always to be vigorous and well nourished, or else dead. Nature's methods of eliminating disease and injury, and with them the suffering they cause, may seem harsh in our eyes, but they are undeniably effective, and where the conscious apprehension of death is, as far as we can see, absent or only momentary, they could scarcely be more merciful, given that pain in one form or another is inevitable in a world which is necessarily imperfect. The wild animals certainly look happier than we do.

11. Many of the ancient practices have in fact become superstitions in the proper sense of the word, and that perhaps is why they no longer seem to be effective (an instance would be the regulation of sowing and planting by the phases of

Our ancestors no doubt realized, consciously or unconsciously or semi-consciously, that there is no end to the complexities and the subtleties of the relationships between living things, so that they are beyond the power of the human brain alone to resolve. Our ancestors were not overweeningly inquisitive about their environment, having been taught by their religions and traditions to accept their human situation. The justification of all such teaching is that the direct and unelaborated human experience provides as much as, and more than, most people can comprehend. Too wide a range of enquiry can distract attention from experiences which, though outwardly simple and even commonplace, are symbolically adequate to provide a support for spiritual needs.[12]

The surface of an expanding sphere moves away from the center which is the principle of its sphericity, and at the same time, as the surface expands, its constituent parts move away from one another. Such is the image of all outward-looking and peripheral knowledge; in becoming more extensive its constituent parts move away from each other and away from their common principle.[13] In this analogy the surface of the sphere represents the visible universe, the world of appearances with which alone modern science is concerned, while the whole sphere, surface included, represents reality as a whole, centered on unity. The surface is indefinite in extent; it has no boundaries, and no part of it is principial with respect to any other. A search for truth confined to the surface can have no finality. If finality is sought in the surface, the search for it inevitably becomes

---

the moon). The attitude of ancient man towards Nature was probably one of a more or less non-analytical acceptance, accompanied by a sense of reverence for the wonderful works of God, a reverence too often caricatured nowadays as 'nature-worship'.

12. An excessive inquisitiveness concentrates attention on matters the outward complexity of which creates an illusion of comprehensiveness, although in reality they are concerned only with appearances, and are therefore superficial.

13. What, one wonders, is the reality underlying modern astronomical theories of an expanding universe? To what extent do they reflect the purely outward-looking tendencies of the modern mentality? It is perfectly possible that the physical universe should appear to be expanding when looked at from a particular point of view, necessarily limited but not necessarily illegitimate; whereas from a different point of view, no less legitimate but perhaps less limited, it would appear otherwise.

more and more extensive and fragmented. The resulting multiplicity and diversity are represented as an enrichment, but it is a false and ultimately harmful enrichment because it is more and more quantitative and out of touch with the purely qualitative center.

The apparent need for experimental research grows rapidly as the field covered by observation grows. Each single experiment can cover only an ever smaller fraction of that field. The approach of science, being experimental, is the approach of trial and error, that is to say, it is purely empirical. If it be true that sound practice, in agriculture or in anything else, can be established on no other foundation, it follows that inquisitiveness and inventiveness are the true measure of intelligence. If that be so, the intelligence of our ancestors was indeed inferior to our own. One must then envisage the recent occurrence of a change in the power of the human brain so great, so rapid and so world-wide that no theory of evolution conceived as a gradual process of adaptation could possibly account for it.[14] What has really happened is that a change of outlook, which can take place without the acquisition of any new powers, has brought about so many changes in our lives that it has been mistaken for an acquisition of new powers.

We have chosen the direction in which we want to go, and we have arrived at a point at which the only hope for the future seems to lie in the extension and acceleration of research, so that changes in the chosen direction may take place more and more quickly. This acceleration is extremely bad for agriculture, and if it is bad for agriculture it is bad for humanity.

The soil, animals and plants have a limited range of adaptability, and adaptation is slow within that range. When the process of forcing up output has reached a certain point, it will have gone too far.

---

14. It could only be accounted for as being something like what biologists call a mutation; but it would be a mutation of a magnitude and a universality to which our present knowledge can suggest no parallel.

A Glance at Agriculture 105

By then it will be too late. Nobody can say what that point is, because before any innovation has had a chance of a fair trial, and before the creatures involved—men included—have had a chance to adapt themselves to it, it has already been superseded by another. There is no chance at all of assessing or anticipating long-term effects, simply because they can only be assessed at the end of a long term; there is simply not time to take more than the most obvious and immediate effects into account.

The one thing we know about these long-term changes is how complex and unpredictable they are, and that they are often irreversible, as for instance in the case of soil erosion. Any attempt to predict their nature is mere guesswork. So far the dangers seem to be, in the soil, loss of texture and trace element deficiencies, in animals and plants liability to diseases and to genetic troubles, and in agriculture as a whole, invasions of weeds and pests. So far, and up to a point, science has been more or less able to keep pace with tendencies in these directions as the need has arisen, but new problems arise ever more quickly. All this emphasizes the growing dependence of agriculture on a complicated and vulnerable scientific and industrial organization over which it has little control.

Perhaps this is the place to mention the recent development of the relatively new science of genetics, which offers possibilities of the artificial production of what would be in effect new species of plants and animals. So far most of its work has been confined to inducing variations in existing species or hybrids by the selection and combination of existing genes, but the production of artificial genes has been seriously propounded. Whether something of that kind is possible or not, future developments are sure to be much more far-reaching than present achievements. We have good reason to know how potentially dangerous to living creatures experiments on the structure of atoms can be. What then, of experiments on the genetic constitutions of creatures themselves? The unintentional production of uncontrollable monstrosities, though they might be no larger than viruses, cannot be ruled out. A discovery that would be described journalistically as a 'major break-through' is greatly to be feared, if only because it would encourage the attribution to humanity of a new 'creative' power. A greater and more insidious danger may be a qualitative deterioration in the animals and plants with which we are so closely associated.[15] And will such experiments always be confined to plants and animals? Experiments on the human constitution itself are not likely to be long deferred.

In looking at the picture of modern agriculture as a whole, and more particularly at the factor of acceleration that dominates it, it is difficult to see how a severe crisis can be avoided, or even postponed for very long. It is impossible to predict the form it might take, chiefly because its proximate cause might not be internal to agriculture. It might for example be connected with its loss of independence and self-sufficiency. It might also be connected directly or indirectly with the growth of world population. It is not at all difficult to envisage a situation in which the demand for cheap food had been replaced by a demand for food at any price. There would then still be pressure, perhaps fiercer even than it is now, and it would certainly be even more quantitative and even less qualitative. The nature of any future crisis is impossible to foresee; but insofar as it affects agriculture as a whole, it will affect every man on earth. Meanwhile, in Britain an average of 50,000 acres of agricultural land are being permanently alienated for other purposes every year.

---

15. Our association with plants and animals is one of mutual dependence. Our dependence for survival on the plants is total, our dependence on the animals is less so, though in practice it is real enough; in both cases the quantitative aspect is more evident than the qualitative, although we ignore the latter at our peril. The plants and animals on the other hand, except for the cultivated species and varieties, are not physically dependent on us in the same way; they could survive if we were to disappear. Scientifically speaking, to say that the dependence of the plants and animals on man is of a spiritual order means nothing, because science is not equipped to take account of that order; nevertheless it is the truth, and therefore must be stated. The function of humanity is essentially spiritual and mediatorial and it is exercised on behalf of the whole creation. When it is neglected the whole creation suffers. Therefore the plants and animals will bear witness against this generation of men in the day of judgment, despite all our societies for the conservation of Nature and for the prevention of cruelty.

One of the forms such a crisis might take is that of what used to be called an 'Act of God'; for instance, it might be precipitated by a readjustment of the earth's crust. It is worthwhile to remember that, in the days when unpreventable disasters were attributed specifically to God, it was at the same time customary to thank Him for benefits received. The two attitudes combined represent an acknowledgment of dependence on God, good for the soul. It is good for the soul because it keeps it in touch with reality. Nothing is worse for the soul because nothing is more false, than any assumption of its independence of God in matters great or small. If in the past disasters were 'acts of God', they are so still; if they were then 'judgments' they are so still. This we admit involuntarily when we use the word 'crisis', the literal meaning of which is 'judgment'.[16]

Both the soul of man and the crust of the earth are subject to God's over-riding dispositions and to His judgments. The world including its inhabitants is multiple, but by virtue of its origin in the divine Unity it constitutes a unity. Whatever may affect one part affects the whole, and whatever affects the whole affects every part. That being so, it would be strange if changes in the crust of the earth and in human mentality were mutually independent. It is not so much a case of a change in one causing a change in the other, as of their proceeding from a common cause. All things move together, towards the fulfillment of the plan of the Great Architect of the Universe, and are interrelated at all stages and not only in their critical or explosive or conspicuous phases. Preparatory phases may not be recognized as such. They may be imperceptible in the case of changes in the earth's crust, while at the same time evident in human affairs, wherein they can be 'signs of the times' to anyone who can read them.

The accomplishment of any phase may be a disaster from the human point of view, not least when it is accompanied by a terrestrial upheaval. We forget that a terrestrial upheaval, though it is a death from the point of view of what precedes it, is a birth from the

---

16. That the course of events in these days should be made up of a succession of 'crises' following one another ever more closely, is probably more significant than most people seem to think.

point of view of what follows it. The world, or a world, is reborn, and it is reborn on a new soil more fertile than that of the ancient worn-out lands. And if the cataclysm is a divine judgment so far as the preceding humanity is concerned, it can also be the divine inauguration of a new humanity, restored to its Edenic state because no longer remote from a direct divine intervention and forgetful of it. And so a new cycle begins, and somewhere in its course an agriculture of some kind will become necessary, as it did with Adam.

Science agrees with religion concerning the periodical occurrence of terrestrial cataclysms, but the two differ profoundly concerning their implications.[17] Science can only see a way out for man through a hypothetical enlargement of his inventiveness, whereby the even more hypothetical opportunities for a human life on the terrestrial pattern afforded by the stellar universe might be opened up to exploration and exploitation.

Religion offers a release of an entirely different kind. It is a release from all entanglements, physical or otherwise, and man can only find it in the unchanging Center of his own being, and of all being, wherein the Spirit dwells eternally and by its radiation confers on all that is peripheral whatever qualitative excellence it may possess.

If we seem to have wandered at times rather far from agriculture, it is because agriculture cannot be considered in isolation and at the

---

17. The Hindu cosmology takes full account of the succession of cycles through which every 'world' and every humanity passes on the way to its final reintegration in the Absolute. The first chapter of the Book of Genesis and the New Testament (in particular the 24th chapter of St Matthew's Gospel and the Book of Revelation) appear to be concerned only with the cycle in which the present humanity is involved; nevertheless, since every cycle, whether great or small, is a manifestation of universal laws, all cycles are basically analogous; the Biblical statement is therefore of more general application than it may at first sight appear to be. In other religions the point of view may be different, but in every case there is an adaptation of a comprehensive truth to the particular mentality of the people to whom the message is addressed. The message is always essentially the same.

same time realistically. It is the principal expression of our relation to Nature, far more so, for instance, than any aesthetic or sentimental relationship; it is woven into the texture of our whole existence and touches us at every point.

From our creaturial point of view, there is God and there is Nature and there is also man, whose body and mind are one with Nature, but who is made in the image and likeness of God. Man is thus by appointment mediator between God and Nature. Man cannot exercise his mediatory function effectively if he allows his gaze to wander from the God who appointed him to it and who is always present to guide him if he will look for guidance. If he uses his God-given dominion over Nature, not in view of God, but of his own aggrandizement, he soon finds himself lonely and insignificant, vainly struggling against the forces of Nature. In the end even his own powers are turned against himself.

Nature manifests in change the changeless dispositions of the Almighty God. Nature has no choice. We have a choice, and we have exercised it in a manner and up to a point at which there seems to be no escape from the involvements it has brought upon us. The industrialization of agriculture is one of those involvements, and it may well prove to be not the least of them.

VIII
Old Age

Anyone who has lived for three score years and ten is old in years. He may try to think and to behave as if the greater part of his life did not lie unalterably in the past, but to do so is a refusal to face the truth. That truth will eventually be forced on him by an undeniable deterioration in his physical and mental powers.

If the whole worth of man resides in his physical and mental powers, old age is no more than a regression culminating in their total extinction. In that case the best that the individual can do for himself is to defer for as long as possible any admission of the inevitable, even to himself. The best that society can do for him is to postpone the inevitable for as long as possible and meanwhile to do all it can to make the decline as little uncomfortable as possible.

Let it be said at once that, since human physical and mental powers have their place and their value in the world, so also have the individual and social attitudes and reactions mentioned. They are not the only possible reactions, but they are the modern reactions, almost to the exclusion of any others. They are not to be despised, but they are incomplete, for they contribute nothing towards the resolution of the perennial problem of life and death, indeed they do not pretend to do so. It is for that reason that by themselves they are unsatisfying.

Birth, life and death are inseparable. The significance of birth and life cannot sensibly be considered apart from that of death. To consider life as a sequence of events while thrusting aside as far as possible the only absolutely predictable and absolutely conclusive event associated with it as firmly as birth is unrealistic. It is impossible to understand life without understanding death. Old age stands as it were between the two, to be understood or misunderstood accordingly. It must be accepted if it comes, and, when it is understood, that acceptance is positive and can be fruitful; but when it is not understood acceptance is negative and resentful and cannot be fruitful.

In these days old age and death seem to be regarded as nothing more than the greatest and the most ineluctable of all the many misfortunes that mar the enjoyability of human life. Their acceptance is therefore negative and resentful. A considerable proportion of the material and scientific resources of society is devoted to the alleviation of the incapacities of old age and to the postponement of death. An indefinite postponement is even mentioned as an ideal not at present attainable, but as a not impossible final triumph of science.[1] This aversion from old age and death, together with the substitution of pity for respect towards the aged, is closely connected with the over-valuation of youth now so prevalent. Youth represents promise, but rarely does it represent anything that can be called attainment. It ought to be valued and treated accordingly.

If a completed individual life does not amount to something that can be called attainment, that life has been lived in vain. If the world as such is considered to be the supreme or the only reality, and if therefore death is a total extinction, the attainment of the individual can only be assessed in terms of the tangible residual effects on the world of his action. Of him it can perhaps be said that he has made his mark in the world, or has made a name for himself, or has made two blades of grass grow where one grew before. An aspiration towards an attainment of that kind is not unworthy in itself, but when there is no higher aspiration it cannot satisfy the deepest needs of the soul, because everyone knows in his heart, whether it be through the teaching of religion or of science or of common sense, that all the works of man will sooner or later be overwhelmed

---

1. Incidentally, it is inconsistent to combine this attitude and these aims with an acute worry about over-population and at the same time the attachment of a high value to the qualities of young children. (How many people would say that without a proper proportion of young children life would not be worth having?) But that is only one of many inconsistencies characteristic of modern society, or one of the many apparent *impasses* with which it is faced.

and lost in some kind of 'end of the world', much as the works of all extinct civilizations have been lost. A few people may try to console themselves by imagining that modern civilization represents such a 'break-through' as to be immune from disasters of that order, but its present state does not afford much encouragement to that belief. Instinctively we know that all that is temporal really is temporal. Even the tangible residual effects of all actions must therefore perish, be they great or small, good or bad. Instinctively we know this, and instinctively we react, for we are not satisfied with an aim directed solely to what is known to be perishable, even though it may be relatively desirable. We seek the imperishable, the eternal, the absolute, because it is our nature to do so; the urge to do so is universal and cannot be without foundation.

According to the traditional view of the situation of man in the Universe the universality of this urge needs no explanation. Scientific man, with his different view of that situation, usually tries to explain it as the outcome of an unrealistic wishful thinking. Anyone who accepts the traditional view in its entirety must also accept the prospect of an end of the world in the form of a 'judgment'. That prospect is at least as terrifying as a prospect of extinction. Indeed to anyone with any imagination it is more terrifying, and a belief in total extinction may then provide an easy way out. One suspects that not a few people prefer to believe in extinction for that reason; they are too lazy-minded to face eternity, despite their instinctive dissatisfaction with temporality.

The traditionally-minded must face eternity, and accept the implications of doing so. Those implications include an acceptance of the inevitability of a judgment which, in relation to our terrestrial life, is situated in the future. They must also include some sort of vision of the universe and of man's place in it *sub specie aeternitatis*.[2] That vision is not accessible directly to a vast majority, for whom eternity is not the everpresent reality it in fact is. By that majority eternity is usually confused with perpetuity, which is simply an indefinite period of time. Eternity transcends time. Anyone who is sufficiently traditionally minded knows that a participation in this

---

2. Which may be roughly translated 'from the point of view of eternity.'

'point of view of eternity' is what distinguishes the prophets, saints and sages of the past from other people. In this lies the secret of their powers to move the hearts of men, not so much by argument as by way of a direct contact with the urge that lies more or less hidden or suppressed in all men, and shows itself in an ingrained dissatisfaction with temporality and a thirst for the changeless. And so, for the ordinary man, that is to say, for almost every one of us, 'facing eternity' implies above all accepting the guidance of those prophets, saints and sages. Thus we get back to tradition. Tradition, at least in its origins, covers every aspect of life. Our present concern is only with the aspect represented by old age.

Traditionally old age is a benediction, and the excellence of its special potentialities is recognized. Anyone to whom old age has been granted has been granted a period when less of the work of the world is demanded of him, when he has fewer responsibilities (real or imagined); it is a time when passions are less insistent, when calm, patience and detachment are less difficult to achieve; a time in which withdrawal from the world and contemplation are natural, so that attainment can be stripped of superfluities, integrated and concentrated, and, by the Grace of God, sanctified.

Spiritual attainment alone is here in question; the time for worldly attainment is past. Spiritual attainment cannot be measured by any human standard, nor is it dependent on the particular nature of the activities of youth or of maturity, provided that those activities have been necessary and have been accomplished as well as they could be. If the soul has in it any spiritual potentiality, old age is the time for the strengthening and firm establishment of that potentiality, so that the soul may be ready for the impending transformation; ready for that passage out of the world of forms which we call death.

By turning this period to good account the aged person is not benefiting himself alone, he is also exercising the function in the world that is most appropriate to his condition. No human function is more indispensable. It is the providential function of the old, who in exercising it find their place in a traditional society, where the excellence of their function is recognized. In a modern progressive society the essential function of the old is not recognized and accordingly they have no real place.

From the 'point of view of eternity', and therefore that of tradition, nothing counts in the end but the quality of the soul. That quality has been manifested in the terrestrial life of the individual; it has been as it were projected into the forms, both corporeal and psychic, which constitute the living being. Alone those forms are transitory, as are all forms, but the qualities that animate them are not so; there is no reason why they should be, for a quality is what it is and remains so, independently of its manifestation. The form of the individual perishes, but what may be called his 'qualitative constitution' remains, no doubt to be projected again into a world of forms subject to conditions other than those that characterize our world, and therefore not imaginable by us.

But these are all only words. Sometimes a truth is communicated more fully and more vividly by its enactment than by words. Such, for instance, is no doubt the significance of the traditional 'transformation scene' in a pantomime,[3] itself a survival of a very ancient form of dramatic art. But the transformation scene has lost its significance, concurrently with the widespread obscuration of the truth it embodies, so no wonder it is dropping out and being replaced by mere fantasies, just as are the traditional fairy stories. The passage into a different world symbolized in the transformation scene is, from the point of view of that world, a birth.

From the 'point of view of eternity' birth and death are one. The fact that old age is from a terrestrial point of view a decline is neither here nor there. What, then, of that clinging to the pleasures of life so commonly regarded nowadays as the only available compensation, for the incapacities of old age? In such an atmosphere nothing but pity is left for the aged, and they, like anyone else, do not want to be pitied. The fault lies with a society that fails to see that

---

3. Transformation scenes such as: Cinderella—slave to princess; Snow White—dead to alive; Sleeping Beauty—asleep to awake. ED.

those who are granted the opportunity afforded by age to prepare for their transformation are blessed, and that their benediction could be reflected back on to the society as a whole. Not, of course, that the aged are the only people who are blessed; others may be no less so, for instance by a high spiritual attainment (in youth or maturity) or by being granted a death that is in a real sense sacrificial; but a discussion of that aspect of the matter here would take us too far from our subject.

The important thing is that the opportunities afforded by old age should not be missed. That is why, for instance, in traditional civilizations, particularly in the East, the care of aged parents is an overriding duty that must be undertaken whatever the sacrifice involved may be. To neglect it is a matter for the deepest shame; the idea of allowing an aged parent to be cared for by anyone else, and particularly by the State, is horrifying. The natural ties between parent and child make the latter more suited than anyone else could be to undertake this care, but in addition their mutual affinity favors the reflection on the child of the blessedness of the parent's state. Often no doubt these ideals are not realized to the full, or even at all, in every case, but the principle is there, and the machinery for its implementation in a traditional society is there.

How remote such ideas are from those prevalent today! It would be tedious to point the contrast in detail. Nowadays people are retiring from work or business earlier and earlier, largely thanks to public and private pension schemes, while death is postponed, thanks to new medical techniques. So-called advanced civilizations are faced with old age as a problem; there is even a new branch of medical science called 'gerontology'. If an increasing percentage of the population are superannuated, what are they going to do with themselves? How can boredom and futility be kept away?

The modern outlook on old age is based on assumptions concerning the purpose of life and the destiny of man totally different from those prevalent in traditional societies. The aged are now valued, if at all, for what they have done or are believed to have done, and not for what they are; their potentiality is supposed to have been exhausted; the potentiality they possess by virtue of their age itself is not recognized as such, and is therefore not valued. Even if it were recognized as a potentiality of sanctification—that being the shortest way of stating what it is—one cannot help wondering to what extent it would be valued. For 'sanctity' is a very unscientific term. Its nature cannot be precisely specified for the reason that it is not of this world (or not wholly of this world, since it has a human aspect).

For those who are granted a long life death is not abrupt. Their final departure from the world is but the culmination of a long process; their detachment from the world is gradual, both physically and psychically, and in the course of it they become less and less 'of this world'. The very young are not yet fully of this world, the aged are in process of becoming less so. From God we came, and to God we must return. May those who are granted a gradual return be granted also the grace to turn it to good account.

IX

'With God all things are possible'

The very existence of our universe, in its fullest extension in space and in time, and with all that it contains both quantitative and qualitative, proves that it is among the things that are possible with God. It is gratuitous to assume that nothing else is possible with God simply because nothing else is at present accessible to us.

Our universe is governed by certain conditions, the chief of which are form, number, time, space and mass or energy, and our faculties are adapted to these conditions and not to any others. If we choose to assume that no other conditions exist or are possible, we are simply assuming that there is nothing beyond what is, in fact or in principle, within the grasp of human perception or the powers of deduction of the human mind. That, if you come to think of it, is a curiously presumptuous thing to do. It makes human limitations the measure of the power of God. It is also curiously naive to behave as if the mind of man, without the help of anything to raise it above its inherent and obvious limitations, could be supposed to be capable of comprehending (in the double sense of enclosing and understanding) not only all that is, not excepting its own self, but also all that is possible. The power of God, as our text states so clearly, comprehends all possibility. All possibility is infinitely more than all actuality, and we can never perceive more than a small fraction even of actuality, let alone of possibility.

The word 'infinitely' has just been used, but not carelessly or conventionally. Once one has abandoned the idea that possibility is limited by the conditions of our terrestrial experience, there is no conceivable reason to assign any limit to it whatsoever. This is exactly what our text says in apparently very simple words. Here, as always, the simplest wording is the least restrictive and the best adapted to convey a highly comprehensive and far-reaching conception. By reason of its very simplicity it contains in potentiality more than any prolonged explanatory statement could convey.

A true statement made in theological terms, as this one is, necessarily corresponds to a truth that can be stated in metaphysical terms. In this case that truth could be called the illimitation of all-possibility. The choice of terms is a matter of opportunity alone.

The metaphysical conception of all-possibility and its illimitation is fundamental. Once it is grasped it does not matter so much what it is called, since all terms are limitative, and here it is a question of an absence of limits. The conception of all-possibility is in fact logically inescapable, for if possibility were limited it would have to be limited by something, and that something would itself be a possibility, for if it were not a possibility, it would be pure nothingness, and so could not be the cause of a limitation (or of anything else).

The conception of all-possibility cannot be grasped at all unless the mind can be freed, at least to some extent, from habits of thought arising from its confinement within the body, which tend to limit its range to the phenomena of terrestrial experience. Language in particular, the means whereby we communicate our thoughts, is derived entirely from our terrestrial experience, and for that reason no verbal statement of the metaphysical theory of all-possibility can convey its full content, or can be intrinsically complete and unequivocal. That fact by no means invalidates the theory, it is only a consequence of its comprehensiveness.[1] Nevertheless, a little further explanation must be attempted.

Every identifiable or definable possibility, whether it be simple or complex, that is to say, every object, every event and every combination of the two, is limited by the fact that there are other possibilities distinct from it and external to it. If that were not the case, it would not be in any way distinguishable in itself, for by definition

---

1. For an exposition of the theory of all-possibility, the reader must be referred to two works by René Guénon: *The Symbolism of the Cross* and *The Multiple States of the Being* (Ghent, NY: Sophia Perennis, 2001).

no possibility is external to all-possibility, which is therefore not limited by any possibility.

It might however be thought that impossibility, being as it were the opposite of possibility, must be distinct from all-possibility and external to it, or in other words that possibility ends where impossibility begins. But impossibility does not begin anywhere, it is another word for 'nothing', a mere conception, purely negative, denying everything that has been or is or could be. Entities have beginnings and ends, total non-entity has neither. If impossibility has no beginning, possibility has no end. Definable entities, insofar as they are considered as existing in their own right, by virtue of what they seem to be rather than by virtue of what they obviously are not, can be regarded as so many limitations of all-possibility. From that point of view their existence represents a sort of departure from all possibility, as it were a step in a 'descent' towards impossibility, which however can never be reached, as the word itself implies. Such a point of view is admissible, and can be useful provided that it is recognized as partial and provisional. It is no more than that because nothing exists in its own right, but only by virtue of its participation in all-possibility. In the last analysis, all-possibility, being limited neither by possibility nor by impossibility, is limitless. As such it is neither definable nor imaginable, since there is nothing outside it to supply either the likeness or the contrast on which identification depends.

For these or similar reasons many people, especially those who pride themselves on being practical or up-to-date, would say that the conception of all-possibility is unnecessary, or at least that it is a purely mental conception embodied in a play of words having no relevance to the solution of current problems, and that therefore the question of its inescapability or otherwise is purely academic. Yet if the conception corresponds to a truth that is fundamental to an understanding of the nature of existence it cannot be negligible. On the contrary, it is vital that it should be grasped by all who are capable of doing so, at least to some extent and in one form or another, whether metaphysical or religious. One of its religious forms is that enshrined in our text. Moreover, since the conception cannot be fully grasped by the mind alone, but involves the whole man, heart as well as mind, the simplicity and directness of that text is very significant.

The physical universe that affects our senses can be regarded as a single complex possibility, that is to say, as a system that can be identified and in principle described. We spend a lot of time trying to formulate its laws, which amounts to defining its limits as precisely as we can. Independently of how far we succeed, the simple fact that the universe is subject to laws, and that its possibilities are limited by those laws, proves that it does not coincide with all-possibility, that is to say that it is not infinite and not alone, and that there is something external to it. That being so, what can be conceived as being external to it other than the indefinity of possibilities postulated by the theory of all-possibility? Any other assumption is arbitrary—this one has an impregnable logical foundation. It is true that it cannot be verified by observation; but neither can any other more limited assumption, since nothing outside our universe can be accessible to observation by us, who, for so long as we rely exclusively on our powers of observation and deduction, are looking at the universe from within and can by no means survey it from without.

Man, and man alone, can recognize the fact that the universe he knows is subject to laws. He fails to make the right deductions from this fact, and so tends to identify the universe with all-possibility. He is tempted to do so more and more as the extent of his knowledge of its observable features increases.

Surely it is evident that more ancient views of the nature of the universe, such as would usually be called 'religious' or 'traditional', although on the physical side less extensive and often less accurate, were really much more comprehensive. At least they took into account possibilities far more extensive than those comprised in our terrestrial state. Furthermore it must not be forgotten that all our means of communication are derived from our common terrestrial experience, so that the nature of wider possibilities can only be conveyed symbolically and never descriptively. The various images made use of to represent them cannot therefore be expected to coincide formally.

Modern scientific knowledge reveals much that was previously unknown, yet it conceals or supplants much more. In aiming at completeness in one aspect of the picture it suppresses the picture as a whole.

Man's awareness of the limitations of his universe implies that there is something in him that can penetrate beyond its bounds, that is to say, beyond the world of phenomena, although his powers of observation can never do so, however well developed they may be.[2] It is just this possibility of seeing the limitations of this world that marks the uniqueness of man and enables him to rise above his terrestrial limitations. When he fails to take advantage of that possibility by neglecting or rejecting the divine revelations which alone can shed light on the mystery of existence—a mystery which is beyond the reach of his natural or unaided mind and senses—he becomes no more than a thinking animal, subject to the same laws as the animals, and having no superior rights save those arising from his superior ingenuity. Hence the universal concern of religious doctrines with a certain detachment from the world as a necessary condition for the realization of man's true destiny.

Our universe, being subject to definable laws, excludes anything that is incompatible with those laws. It can be regarded as a system of mutually compatible possibilities, or 'compossibles' as they can conveniently be called. The compossibles constituting a system such as our universe are not assembled by chance nor by any arbitrary choice, they simply constitute a system because they are what they are. The number of possible systems is indefinite, not only because the number of possibilities that can be assembled into systems is indefinite, but also because any given possibility can form part of a plurality of different systems, each of which is defined by a unique set of conditions, and has its own relative internal unity, and its own relative reality. The reality of each is however derived entirely from its participation in all possibility, which alone is absolutely real and wholly itself. Whatever else may be or may not be, all-possibility cannot not be. The one thing that is inconceivable is its limitation.

---

2. It may be mentioned in parentheses that phenomena such as are sometimes called 'paranormal' are still phenomena, and as such they are of this world, and, as with normal phenomena, their outward form is one thing and the interpretation of its significance is another.

All the rest follows. It is vain to seek to formulate the ultimate reason why things are what they are; they are what they are because it is possible that they should be so, and therefore impossible that they should not be so; and they are in a particular system—our own universe for instance, because they are compatible with the conditions that define that system. In theological terms one could say that they are what they are and where they are because God made them so and gave them their place. If that sounds a bit old-fashioned, it is nonetheless much better sense than a good deal that is said today about the origin and nature of our universe.

All the above is scarcely as much as a sketch of the theory of all-possibility. It may however be just enough to convey by contrast some idea of the complete inadequacy of the modern scientific outlook, which equates what man can see and know with the whole of reality. In attributing a sort of absolute validity to this outlook, scientific man is taking a fraction of a fraction to be unity. At the same time he is making himself insignificant, a mere trivial accident in the evolutionary process of an apparently arbitrary and purposeless mechanism. For so long as he continues to try to squeeze reality into the miserably inadequate vessel of his own brain he will continue himself to become more and more insignificant.

A living terrestrial being, a human being for example, can, like the universe itself, be regarded as a coherent system of compossibles, an assemblage of inter-related potentialities, manifested in a mode which accords with the conditions that characterize this universe. Those potentialities constitute an individual being distinct from all others because they are what they are and for no other reason; as in the case of the universe, their assembly is in no sense fortuitous or arbitrary; and they remain for ever what they are, whether manifested or not. They can be manifested under a variety of conditions without losing their cohesion, their individuality, because its source is in their intrinsic nature and is not external to it. Their manifestation under particularized conditions, for instance those peculiar to our universe, realizes only such potentialities as are concordant with those conditions, but not others, so that it appears both as a realization and as a limitation. The total being in all its potentiality is not realized, but only as it were one possible aspect of it. A different aspect, perhaps less limited, perhaps more so, must characterize its manifestation under other conditions, but the total being must remain what it was and is.

Only in a total release from all the limitations inherent in manifestation can the being realize its full potentiality. In more familiar words, man has an immortal soul capable of perfection, and its sojourn on this earth is but a partial and passing phase. On this earth we have a body, but it is not ourselves, it belongs to this universe, wherein it reflects potentialities inherent in our being. At death we leave this universe and are therefore parted from our bodies, but this does not affect our real being and its potentialities, which can and must be then reflected in some other 'universe' in a new mode, according to whatever conditions may prevail. These may include some kind of duration and extension, corresponding to, but not identifiable with, our time and space, as well as something corresponding to the 'materiality' that conditions our bodies, but such possibilities are far beyond the range of our imagination. St Paul says of our bodies, 'It is sown a natural body, it is raised a spiritual body. There is a spiritual body and a natural body.'[3] The doctrine of the resurrection of the body gives rise to many doubts and difficulties, even in the minds of believers. It need not do so, since the possibilities manifested in the body cannot be annihilated.

In our present state we are involved in time and space, wherein possibilities are manifested in succession and in extension; but they can equally well be considered as co-existing in a non-temporal and non-spatial state (although this does not come naturally to us because of our present involvement in time and space). Our present viewpoint is not for that reason false or distorted, but it is particularized in a special way. The fact that a more generalized conception can be reached, at least by some people, is direct evidence of our situation on the central and 'vertical' axis connecting the whole

3. 1 Cor. 15:44.

hierarchy of possible states, each of which can be envisaged as a 'horizontal' expansion of a point on this axis. Such a picture of our situation is evidently symbolical; as such, its content is virtually inexhaustible.[4]

Sometimes it may be helpful to think of the present as permanent and as alone wholly real. In it alone can we act or be acted upon; it summarizes the past and conditions the future; it alone is always with us, it is stationary while events move past it; it will still be when everything else has gone; it is the container, events are its ever-changing content.

Comparably, space is spherical, and a sphere is defined by the relation of its parts to its center; it may revolve or expand or contract, but always by reference to its center, which contains and regulates all its potentiality. In the terrestrial state the symbol (the likeness) of eternity is the present, and the symbol of infinity is the dimensionless center, the point. The present is eternal, the center is ubiquitous.

Eternity is not a very long time, nor is infinity a very capacious space. And in the last analysis eternity and infinity are not two, but one, and all-possibility is one of the names of that indivisible Unity.

Let us return again to theology and consider what religion teaches. Being concerned with humanity alone, for the good reason that humanity represents the central and only fully conscious element in the universe, religion is only indirectly concerned with the multiple states of being as they affect non-human entities, animate or inanimate. All living beings 'have the same religion as ours' as Black Elk says of the birds,[5] that is to say, they express their dependence on God each in its own way, in their forms and their behavior (see also

---

4. *The Symbolism of the Cross* (see note 1) is mainly concerned with the development of this symbolism.

5. *Black Elk Speaks*, by John G. Neihardt (Lincoln: Univ. of Nebraska Press, 1961), p199.

for example Ps. 19:1–3, and 104:21). Having little or no consciousness of their individuality they are not tempted to the sort of presumption of independence that beguiles us. They have therefore not only no capacity for, but also no need for, anything corresponding to the external forms of religion as we know them.

The doctrines of the great religions are formulated in many different ways and expressed through a very varied imagery, but integral to them is always the idea that the human being has an essential and immortal part which passes through a plurality of states, of which this present life is one. The 'monotheistic' religions teach, for instance, that man has an immortal soul, given to him by God, and destined after its earthly death, in which it is separated from the body, to pass on to Paradise, purgatory or hell, the choice depending on what it has done during its sojourn on earth. This no doubt is a great simplification of the situation in its entirety; nevertheless, it expresses the metaphysical truth adequately, and in a manner adapted to the needs and capacities of the people who are called upon to accept it, for whom it is unnecessary to know more than this. It is however vital for the state of their souls that they should not know less than this, and that they should order their lives accordingly, that is to say, as a preparation for an inevitable change of state.

At death we drop all our terrestrial characteristics, all bodily and mental forms, for they are but the temporary manifestation of the possibilities inherent in and characteristic of the immortal center which is our real being, and that real being takes on another form, reflecting its proper nature in its new surroundings.

While subject to terrestrial conditions (or to any others), the individual being does not become something other than it is in principle or in potentiality, but it is passing through a phase of limitation, as it has done before and will do again. It will be a different phase every time; it has been said that 'we pass this way but once,' and this is necessarily true; the timeless coexistence of all things in all-possibility excludes any repetition, simply because two identical possibilities are not two but one. That is why religion treats the judgment that faces all beings after death as final, for so it is from the point of view of terrestrial existence, which is what a terrestrial religion is primarily concerned with. Religion could not, however, present the truth without taking account of non-terrestrial states: in the monotheistic religions they are referred to as paradises, purgatories and hell, and are situated symbolically 'above' or 'beneath' this world.

It will have become clear that within a given set of conditions or compossibles (in other words, in a particular universe), every possibility compatible with those conditions must be manifested, the universe in question being a manifestation of all-possibility in a particular mode. Therefore possibilities of distinction, of contrast, of definition, also of opposition, contradiction and negation, and even of a sort of apparent negation of itself, cannot be excluded. Manifestation consists precisely in this kind of throwing into relief of one possibility by its separation from another, or by the possibility of its apparent negation, without which everything would remain in the permanent indistinction and non-manifestation of all-possibility itself. But if things were to remain in that state, all-possibility would not be all-possibility, since the possibilities of distinction and opposition, that is to say, of manifestation, would be excluded, and that is impossible. White is manifested through its contrast with black; similarly with good and evil, beauty and ugliness, truth and untruth. In the non-manifestation of all-possibility there is no separateness and no negation (for negation implies a separation), there is only the unimaginable perfection of totality—but we have here already passed far beyond what words alone can convey.

This is the only complete answer to people who say, 'If all things are possible with God, why does not He eliminate evil and ugliness and pain?' There are other answers of course, some good and some bad, but they are all vulnerable in one way or another. If God were to eliminate these things, there would be no manifestation, no world and no salvation; but more than that, there would be no completion, no perfection, no fulfillment.

St Paul says that 'all things work together for good to them that love God.'[6] This is a comprehensive statement of the metaphysical truth in theological terms. We read too in the Book of Genesis[7] that, from the third day of the creation, when the distinctively manifested features of this universe begin to appear, God saw that each of them was good. Finally, he 'saw everything that he had made, and, behold, it was very good'. As in the case of our text, the simplicity and directness of these words confers on them a power and a range that would be diminished by any dialectical expansion or elaboration. As it is with fundamental statements of truth such as these, so it is with faith. A simple and direct faith is stronger and more far-reaching than a faith justified or sustained mainly by philosophical or quasi-philosophical considerations. Insofar as the latter is of the brain alone it is peripheral and mobile. Simple faith is of the heart, it subsists at the center and illumines the whole being, brain and all. With it, philosophy can live, without it, philosophy is a dead thing.

As limited beings, we cannot know all-possibility, still less imagine or visualize it in any way, since it cannot be compared or contrasted with anything, nothing being outside it or separable from it. Yet at the same time the universe we can know is nothing but a reflection or refraction of all-possibility, and derives all its qualities and all its reality therefrom.

St Paul said, 'Now we see through a glass, darkly.'[8] Only if we look upon the universe as a partial refraction of all-possibility, and not as if it were itself identifiable with all-possibility, can we 'see God in all things.' It is just in this sense that He is 'in all things', and that all things subsist only 'in God' and not in themselves. At the same time all things, to the extent that their appearance is taken for the reality, play the part of so many veils, hiding the Presence of Him with whom all things are possible.

---

6. Rom. 8:28.
7. Gen. 1:9 to 31.
8. 1 Cor. 13:12.

Index

Adam 108
Agriculture 1, 92–109

Black Elk 124
Buddha 48, 57

Cambrian fossils 24
Christian(ity) 83, 85, 88–90
Christian(s) 83, 85–86, 90
creation 48, 56, 76, 106 n15, 127
cultivars 50–54

Darwin 50
Darwinian postulate 24
de Chardin, Teilhard 82

eugenics 74
evolution 23–30, 41, 58, 80, 82, 84, 88, 104

factory farming 99–100
Farrer, Reginald 57
flowers, beauty of 40–57
    plastic 55–56

Genesis, Book of 74–76, 108 n17, 127
genetics 105
gerontology 115
Guénon, René 1, 45, 118 n1

Heisenberg 22, 64 n1

Hindu cosmology 108 n17

Koran 77

Lao Tzu 78

MacLean, Prof. R. 13 n5

nihilism 45–46

Old Age 110–116

paleontological 24, 90
predestination & free will 63–78
Russell, Bertrand 41, 45

Saint Paul 123, 127
Schrödinger 22
Schuon, Frithjof 1, 83
Soviet Russia 14 n5
Spirit (*spiritus*) 6–11, 69, 86, 93, 97, 108
symbolism 18, 34, 36
    beauty 44, 52
    flowers 48, 57
    geometrical 36, 90
    religious 35–37, 76

theology 124
Transformist Illusion (Douglas Dewar) 24–25
Trinity 48

www.ingramcontent.com/pod-product-compliance
Lightning Source LLC
Chambersburg PA
CBHW031137090426
42738CB00008B/1120